Undercover:
Becoming Street Smart
In
Central Ohio

Sandra K-Horn

Other books by Sandra K-Horn

Downward Spiral
After the Tears Dry

Undercover: Becoming Street Smart in Central Ohio

Copyright © 2022 by Sandra K-Horn

No part of this book may be used or reproduced in any manner whatsoever without written permission except in the case of brief quotations embodied in critical articles and reviews.

ISBN: 979-8-218-07700-6

To
Michael N. Powell
And
Shawn Bain
For what they have done and continue to do
to Save Lives.

AUTHOR'S NOTE

This book is about real people and real events. Michael N. Powell and Shawn Bain spent countless hours recounting their experiences to make this book possible. Other interviews were conducted to verify events. Newspaper accounts and television footage were also viewed. In some instances, I took liberties with dialogue. All events are portrayed as they happened according to the memories of the individuals interviewed.

Both Michael N. Powell and Shawn Bain checked the manuscript for factual accuracy.

Certain names have been changed to protect privacy. Each pseudonym has been italicized the first time it appears.

Introduction

"The 1980s saw the emergence of cocaine, particularly crack cocaine, as a new focus of concern. After President George Bush's televised address in September 1989 (his first as President) on a national drug control strategy, sixty-four percent of respondents to a New York Times-CBS poll rated drugs as the nation's number one problem (New York Times, 1990). Respondents to such surveys during that period typically rated crime and AIDS as the number two and number three problems—both of which are associated with drugs. As one measure of the importance attached to this issue, in fiscal 1992, the federal government spent twelve billion dollars on anti-drug efforts, and state and local agencies together spent roughly the same amount (White House, 1992)."

It was hard to believe the fight against drugs was already in full operation for the drug enforcement agencies in the 1980 and 90s. This fight against drugs would take place every day all over Ohio by individuals in law enforcement, and especially for the undercover officers in the Drug Task Force of the Franklin County Sheriff's Department.

Working a shift from 6 p.m. to 2 a.m. has its perks and its downsides. Most of the time, Mike Powell would get home about 2:30 in the morning, depending on the night and the length of his reports. There were many nights, even though he was home, he couldn't go to bed. If he had a call to the morgue or saw something that was particularly troubling or even a close call, his mind would not shut off. If he was working a case or supervising a case, he would be troubled about the best way to proceed.

The best perk was he could see his kids. One boy and three girls. His wife worked so he could get them up and make sure they were ready for their day. His wife would leave notes, sometimes as to what the kids needed. If he had to go in early, or in the summer, he took the kids to the babysitter. He also took care to mow the lawn, do yard work, or relax by washing the car. There were even times he would have time to take a nap.

As his schedule varied it would allow him to play basketball with other officers in the winter and softball in the summer. As his kids got older, he could make their events. But the job and his dedication were hard on his family relationships. As in many cases, divorce occurred.

The downside would be once he left home, five days a week, sometimes seven, he would become this fake person. Sometimes he was Eddie; other times, he was Brad. When he worked in a place called The Caravan, he wore old and ragged jeans, and when the conditions were right, a long denim coat. Mike preferred his hair short, but most of the time because he was working undercover, he wore his hair long and sported a mustache. When he wanted to change his look, he grew a beard. Or maybe he wouldn't shave for a week or two. He had his ear pierced so he could wear certain types of earrings for conversation starters. Since he worked a lot of bars where they knew drug trafficking took place, he sported a coke spoon, a skull, or marijuana leaf stud. Not usually one to wear jewelry, but at work, he wore gold necklaces with a gold nugget or the word "snow" dangling. A headband, sunglasses, or a hat, depending on the situation, would complete his look. His partner would laugh because with all this care to look "the part" he would wear an ironed bandana. In the winter, he wore a long coat that would stand out and gain attention. All these props helped give him cover or start a conversation with a possible dealer or user.

Mike walked into the roll call room around two or three in the afternoon (depending on his shift). He would join on the average of ten to twelve other detectives and supervisors.

The sergeant or lieutenant would open the meeting of men and at least three females to relate any issues concerning policy, procedures, or rules and regulations that needed to be reviewed. It was up to each team member to brief everybody else on what was commencing on each case. If they had completed deals the day before, they would discuss how the night went, what went right, or what they missed. The detectives on the case would talk about what they felt the next step might be. Others would advise or agree. Each officer would then report on what he or she would be doing with informants they would contact, or surveillance they would conduct on complaints that were received from the public.

The supervisor (the sergeant or lieutenant) would then decide the primary focuses for the day or week. There were always lag times as each case proceeded. A team could be working on two or three cases at any given time. To add to the challenge, in one case, an undercover could be called Mark, and at the same time, he could be working on another case with the name of Steve. There were also times, an officer would have to lay low for a bit because a case he had been working had become a high-profile news story. He would have to wait until things cooled down to become active on the street again.

Sometimes the whole unit would work on a particular buy that would be considered high risk. These would concern armed and dangerous targets or individuals who had prior convictions for trafficking.

More often, the teams would break up into two or three and hit the streets. Each officer had an assignment for his or her shift.

Michael Powell and Shawn Bain were members of the undercover deputy sheriffs Drug Task Force.

PART ONE

Michael 1970 -1980

Mike's first buy

When Mike Powell became the newest member of the Franklin
County Sheriff's Narcotic Unit, there was very little training for
undercover prospects. For two weeks, he was assigned
surveillance to learn from the veterans. But mostly, it was trial
and error. He was told to come with a sort of script. He had to
choose a fake name. One that he would respond to without
hesitation. He had to come up with what to say if asked to do a
drug, and he had to get a telephone number to use if a
perpetrator had to get a hold of him.

His first drug deal assignment found him scared and feeling
unprepared. LSD was his first buy. Thirty-unit doses. These were
microdot acid, tiny little pills of LSD. The state law at the time
specified that thirty units would bring a mandatory seven-year
jail time but could stretch to twenty-five years.

He had a string of unanswered questions. Who am I buying
from? What do I say if asked if I'm a policeman? What do I say if
I'm asked what I'm going to do with the drugs I'm buying? It was
up to him to come up with the answers.

He was assigned an experienced informant who was being
"paid" to arrange transactions to introduce undercover agents to
traffickers throughout Central Ohio. What threw Mike was his
informant was the son of a policeman in another agency. It was
hard for him to wrap his brain around that a son of a policeman
had been selling drugs. Now his "payment" was buying time off
his sentence. He had to assume the informant knew what an

undercover agent could or could not do. Mike obsessed about these concerns to ramp up his already out-of-control nervousness. What made this all worse for him was he had no experience or knowledge about LSD. He didn't know what it looked like or how a person would even take the drug in this form. He decided the way to cover his inexperience was that he was going to say he was buying it for a friend.

His superior informed Mike he was going to wear a body wire. In the late 70s, early 80s, these transmitters were bulky. What if the dealer wanted to pat him down? How could he not answer then if he was an officer?

Despite his concerns, a wire was taped to his chest. It was a cold November, so on top of the wire Mike wore a tee shirt, a sweatshirt, and over that, a jacket. Self-conscious, he checked several angles in a mirror to make sure the wire couldn't be seen. Looking at the other officers in his unit, he noted the narcotics officers wore their hair long. They also added an earring or two. He hadn't been in the unit long enough, so his hair was still standard officer short. He grabbed an old ball cap and stuck it on his head.

Mike met his informant about a mile and a half from the location they were supposed to make the transaction. Mike wasn't sure what to do when he met him. Do they shake hands? His informant was in his early twenties. About Mike's age.

Mike felt his anxiety ramp up the closer they came to the place the transaction was to go down. He relaxed his hands on the wheel when they stopped at a light. No conversation transpired. They pulled into the parking lot of a Kroger on S. High Street. Mike decided he would pull up by some other cars so they could blend in. It was a midafternoon buy so at least the lighting was still good.

The target was a 25-year-old male who worked as a meat cutter. The informant went inside to let the target know his buyer was here. Mike watched as the informant casually returned to the car. Mike wondered if something had gone wrong. His nerves were at a high pitch. The car door opened, and the informant let Mike know before he asked that the target would be out shortly. As they sat in the car waiting, Mike shifted his weight and straightened his shoulders. His hands remained on the steering wheel. His legs were still. *What if he wants me to test the drug? Know where I work? Where I live?*

Finally, which was probably only a few minutes, Mike saw a man in a blood-streaked butcher's apron come out of the store. The informant got out to let him identify the car. Both men entered the car, the informant in the front, and the target in the back.

Mike said, "You got the acid?"

The meat cutter target said, "You got the money?"

Mike reached into his jacket pocket and pulled out the money. Without turning, he handed it back to him over his left shoulder. A hand with a packet of cellophane appeared over the front seat on his right side. The meat cutter had put the microdots into cellophane that looked like a cigarette package wrapper. Mike knew he should count the microdots, but his hand was shaking so badly the microdots were jumping around like popcorn in their wrapper. He shoved the container in his jacket pocket.

Mike thanked the guy. The guy said thanks back and quickly opened the car door. He started to go back to the store, paused, turned, and then motioned to Mike's informant to join him. The informant looked at Mike. "Go ahead," said Mike, "but don't exchange or get any other product from him."

The informant nodded.

He was there for a small amount of time. Mike had so many thoughts swimming in his brain. *Did he want me to test the drug? Search the car for police stuff?* Both looked casual in their conversation. Mike was antsy, but knew he had to wait.

"So, what did he say?" asked Mike when his informant returned to the car.

"He told me never, ever bring you back again while you're high. Christ, you yelled at him when you asked for the acid. He thought you were on some sort of drug!"

Mike felt like an electrical circuit went through his body. Driving again, he pulled into the agreed meeting place where he knew his back up was waiting. As he parked, he noticed his supervisor and back up guys were standing around their cars, animated and laughing.

Mike placed his vehicle next to another unmarked car and joined the group. "Everything go, okay?"

His supervisor approached and clapped him on the shoulder. "Fine, Mike. But you know you didn't exactly sound like yourself."

"What ya mean?" said Mike.

"Come on, ya gotta listen."

Mike didn't recognize his own voice. It sounded more like his14year-old self. The recording yelled, "Ya got acid?"

The guys congratulated him on his first dope deal. He couldn't believe he had bought real LSD and could be soon charging a guy with a high-level felony. As he wrote up his report, he realized the charge would have to wait. If the guy walked up to him right in front of him at his desk, he wouldn't have been able to identify him.

Vietnam

Brought up in the small town of Delphos, Ohio, he became of age just in time for the Vietnam War. In the graduating class of 1969, the Vietnam War loomed over the psyche of all young men as they graduated from high school. The death and injury statistics were continuously published on the news. His brother-in-law had been drafted and fought on the front lines. Later, standing with his family at his brother-in-law's gravesite listening to Taps, Mike's fear of Vietnam increased.

Mike received his lottery notice of sixty-five. When he signed up for the Air Force on April 1, 1970, he hoped he could avoid Vietnam. After completing his basic training, he received his orders to go to Vietnam.

At nineteen, he learned to shoot fully automatic weapons like the M-16 and the 60-caliber machine gun and crawl under barbed wire as live gunfire zipped over his head. It was surreal to him to use his athleticism that he honed in playing football to throw a grenade accurately. It became real when a Chief Master Sargent told him to pray every day for guidance during the three hundred and sixty-five days he would be in Vietnam. It was the first time he had heard anyone think in terms of days, instead of weeks, months, or years.

Mike took a leave to come home to marry his high school sweetheart. They thought they could make it through anything.

He left for Vietnam in early May 1970 and was assigned to the 377th Combat Group at Tan son Nhut Airbase in Saigon. After ten days, he was moved to Da Nang Airbase, well known as Rocket City because it was bombed so often. Wanting to be awake when the rockets came, Mike hoped to be assigned to night duty.

Mike was assigned to a bunker/tower site. The bunker was pitch dark and surrounded by sandbags. His job was to mind a 60-caliber machine gun. Most of the time, he would end up in the tower with Pedro Bustos, who was senior to him. Together they would watch the perimeter of the base across from the area called the Dogpatch. Most people in The Dogpatch were supporters of the United States. But also in this village were suspected Viet Cong (Charlies) and VC sympathizers. Mike and Pedro would be on constant alert at night for individuals, called zappers who would be dressed in black, skillfully cut the protective barbed wire, and attempt to sneak into the base to kill soldiers and destroy planes.

When the alert for rockets would go off, Mike would beg God to get him through the night. Everyone would hit the bunkers and stay low until the bombing stopped.

The monsoon season was depressing and cold. For long periods, the soldiers would experience rain with no breaks of sunshine. In the bunker, it was wet and bone damp. Other times, when it was warm and quiet, Mike could forget where he was and take in the beautiful nights with the contrasting dark sky and endless depth of bright stars. He stayed on the night shift for about five months before he was reassigned to the day shift.

As a more experienced airman, he would work the gates of entry. The days were okay, but there were many terrifying nights. When the sirens went off to alert everyone rockets were incoming, he would join everyone else in the sandbag bunkers for protection.

Vietnam was beautiful except for the war. Most of the Vietnamese people Mike came to know were friendly. They just wanted their country to be free and neutral. He spent only one year in Vietnam. Spending his twentieth birthday with the war zone of death all around him was unforgettable.

He returned from Vietnam in April 1972. Required to

wear his uniform when flying made him an easy target for people against the war. In Chicago's O'Hare Airport, people looked at him with disgust and shook their heads. They muttered 'baby killer' as he walked by them. He braced for a confrontation when a man walked up to him in the airport store, "Hey, soldier." The man reached out his hand and said, "Thank you for your service."

Relieved, Mike talked to him and found out he was a veteran of WWII.

He was sent to Lockbourne Air Force Base (now called Rickenbacker) outside of Columbus, Ohio. Lockbourne was a top security refueling wing for the Air Force. It had the big KC -135s stationed there. He trained in creating IDs for airman and their families, top-secret background checks, and security.

One individual Mike would get to know, and respect was Rufus Engram. Facing the end of his tour, Mike was at the point where he was deciding if he should re-enlist. Rufus came in and shared he was leaving the Air Force and joining the Franklin County Sheriff's office. They were hiring, and he suggested Mike do the same thing. It was a large police department, and Engram thought it would give him many opportunities.

Mike took the sheriff's department test and was offered a job in mid-November. He accepted and was honorably discharged on December 6, 1973.

Early Days

It was December 10, 1973, when Mike reported to his first assignment with the Franklin County Sheriff's Office (FCSO) working in the County jail. It was his job to take care of the inmates. Some were convicted, others awaiting trial. As he learned in the Air Force serving at Da Nang Airbase, he had to always be aware of his surroundings. Inmates would spit on officers or throw a food tray. Officers were always on guard for assault.

He respected the inmates as people. He learned some inmates understood what he did by following regulations, and others would try to intimidate him and other officers to get what they wanted. Many of the inmates Mike would encounter would be the same people he would meet when he was assigned to patrol. Then, the respect he showed them in jail would be returned. They also, occasionally, would serve as informants on people who committed crimes in the county.

Mike took the Law Enforcement course at the Police Academy and became a certified peace officer. This allowed him to carry a gun and have full arrest powers. He only spent a little over nine months in the jail facility before he was assigned to patrol on the third shift.

After just one week of riding with an experienced officer, his training was complete. His patrol area was busy, well known for a lot of car thefts. He worked from 10:45 p.m. to 7 a.m.

One of the first things Mike did was get to know the business owners and their employees in his district. He wanted the people in the area to know he was there to help. He didn't really like to work traffic violations and averaged maybe five or six tickets a month. But he loved the shift because it was busy. He wanted to work on the felonies, such as burglaries, robberies, car thefts, and assaults. In the district he was assigned, that was no problem.

One early Monday morning Mike was stopped at a traffic light. He noticed a man putting items in a car in front of a room at a local motel. The man kept stopping his task and looking around. After Mike pulled into the motel parking lot, he marked on the radio that he had a suspicious male at the motel's location. He gave dispatch the license number. Mike questioned the man if everything was okay. As the man stood by the police vehicle, the radio squawked,

The car is stolen out of the Cincinnati area. Back up is on the way.

Having heard it, the guy ran back into the room. Gun drawn; Mike chased him. "Come out here with your hands up!"

As the man came out, a backup car arrived with two officers. As one of the officers approached to assist, Mike saw him glance inside the car. Mike cuffed the man and walked him over to the hood of his car. The officer said, "There's another guy in there!"

He tugged the car door open and pulled the second man out of the car. Mike saw the officer's face pale as he yelled, "There's a baby in here!"

All three men froze, at first, aghast. The officer who pulled the door open looked at Mike and said, "The guy was lying face down on the seat. I thought he was asleep!"

The officer handcuffed the second man and pushed him over to his partner. He then reached into the car and picked up the infant and brought the baby's mouth to his ear. "He's breathing."

Calling to Mike, he said, "Call for an ambulance."

Once they secured the area, they called in to find out if there was a missing child report from Cincinnati. They found out that the men had been involved in a domestic dispute in Cincinnati and had stolen the car and the child.

The men were arrested and taken to jail and, eventually, back to Hamilton County to face kidnapping and auto theft charges. They had fled north to Columbus to evade police and then head to Indiana.

For the deputies, the best part was they helped the baby and her mother reunite safely.

***

One Saturday night, Mike reported to roll call before his shift. He was advised that a man by the name of Bobby Woods had robbed and assaulted an elderly lady in the Westland Mall area. The lady visiting from Kentucky was walking back to a motel where she was staying. She was recovering at Doctor's West Hospital. Woods had allegedly thrown her to the ground and injured her. The detective on the case told him felony warrants had been filed on Woods.

Mike knew Woods from his district. As soon as Mike went on patrol, he stopped at several businesses telling his sources (people who trusted and shared information with him) he was looking for Woods.

In the small township of New Rome, New Rome Pizza was a local hangout. Knowing Woods was a frequent customer, Mike stopped in to let the manager, Rick, know he was looking for Woods.

It wasn't a half-hour later when the radio room called Mike to let him know Rick had some information for him. Mike hurried back to the pizza place, parking in the back to avoid anyone seeing his vehicle. In the kitchen among the workers and ovens, Rick told him an Around the World pizza had been ordered. The only person who ordered that type of pizza was Bobby Woods. The pickup order would be ready in fifteen to twenty minutes.

Mike hustled out to the cruiser to alert dispatch. The dispatcher said she would make sure the detective looking for Woods knew. She soon returned the detective's message that he was going to continue to follow his own leads. Undaunted, Mike went back inside and sat down in a booth.

The restaurant was empty except for the manager, one employee, and Mike. A woman came into the pizzeria. Rick nodded to Mike. She was paying for the pizza when Mike slowly approached her. As he spoke, he held his badge low so she could see it. "Ma'am, I know you are picking up that pizza for Bobby Woods."

The woman turned pale, and her hand shook as she gave Rick her money.

"You know, Bobby has committed a felony. If you are hiding him, I can arrest you for aiding a felon."

The woman stood still. She looked at Rick. He took her money, placed it in the cash register and showed her the palms of his hands in a gesture of "it's up to you." She said, "He's out in the car."

"Okay. Good. Stay here inside, or I'll take you in for interfering with Bobby's arrest."

Looking at Rick, Mike said, "Call the radio room. Tell them to send me back up. Woods is here."

Mike peeked out the side door leading to the parking lot. Woods was in the front passenger side of a white GM sedan, watching for the woman to return. Mike slipped his gun out, opened the door, and ran to the car. Woods spotted him and tried to exit the car door. Mike yelled, "Get on the ground, Bobby!"

Slowly, Woods walked away from the car, and his knees buckled. He laid face down on the ground. Keeping his gun on him with his right hand, Mike used his left hand to pull out his cuffs. He cuffed Woods' wrists behind his back. Woods was taller and heavier than Mike, approximately six feet tall, around 185-190 pounds. He probably thought Mike would shoot him if he took off.

Mike was just jerking him into a standing position when back up pulled into the parking lot.

Buy Bust March 1, 1980

Making detective at twenty-seven and being named Officer of the Year in 1978 was something Mike was proud of. He was moved to second shift to cover anything from thefts to assisting in homicides. Working second shift made it difficult to see his kids and wife *Tracy* as much, but he thought they could work it out. They had been sweethearts since high school. He had married her on leave between Air Force Training and going to Vietnam. They had survived that. But the more Mike became absorbed with his work, the more alienated he felt toward his wife. Their marriage suffered and ended. Their youngest daughter was only two.

Mike loved his work. He was always curious why people committed crimes. He had a strong desire to investigate crimes instead of just handing data over to detectives. As he advanced to the Homicide Unit, he worked three to four murders within the year and learned as much as he could from the more experienced detectives. He dealt with the autopsies because he was fascinated by how much the coroner could discover. Mike learned more about the human body during this time than he had in all his schooling and homicide training. His job was to jot notes and take possession of any evidence the coroner found. He became immersed in determining the details of the case, bringing the perpetrator to justice, and giving the family of the victim closure. When he was at work, he was all in. When he was at home, even playing with the kids, his mind was still working on a case.

There was a lot of pressure to cover homicide investigations. It's the job of the team to determine the details of the case, to bring a person to justice, and give closure to the family of the victim.

Mike enjoyed the work until Captain Rob Herdman called him out of bed for a murder suicide. When Mike arrived at the coroner's office, he learned he was there to witness the autopsy of the man who Mike learned was the murderer. He did what he usually did. He sat patiently as the coroner did his autopsy. After the three-hour autopsy, Mike left the laboratory to stretch his legs. He walked back in to see another body on the table, covered with a sheet. Mike could feel his stomach lurch as he absorbed this body was the size of a small child.

"Mike, I've never known you to pass out during an autopsy. Right now, you look like you're about to need smelling salts," said the coroner's assistant.

The coroner walked back into the lab. "You didn't tell me who the guy killed," said Mike.

Mike was told by the coroner that the man killed his two-year-old daughter. "That guy I just examined was a suicide. According to the guys who brought them in he left a note saying the courts were taking her away from him. The guy wrote, 'No way.'"

Mike asked if he could use the phone. He called Captain Herdman to replace him on this autopsy. His own little girl was just three.

That was it for Mike. Captain Herdman called him into his office later that week and suggested Mike might want to look at an opening in the Narcotic Unit.

Mistakes Can Be Deadly

Joe Gordon, one of Mike's first partners in the Narcotics Unit, would be one of his closest friends for twenty-five years. First paired together to provide backup for a raid, Joe and Mike were nervous. They were both rookies in this unit. Detectives were looking for a guy who was dangerous and probably armed. They had received word the perp was in a room on the second floor of a rent-by-the-hour hotel; they just didn't know which one. The rooms were primarily empty in the afternoon, so one team took one side of the hotel, and Mike and Joe took the other. As he approached room 255, Mike heard a floorboard creak. Mike yelled. "Open up, police!"

The door was unlatched. Mike kicked it open and yelled, "Put your hands up, Mother f—er!" He swung around. His gun stretched out. The barrel of his weapon clunked to the floor in front of him.

Time stalled. The burly tattooed man looked at Mike. At the gun barrel. He burst out laughing.

Joe moved around Mike, standing frozen, took one arm of the man, then the other, and cuffed him. The captured man's laughter insulted Mike's ears as Joe read him his rights.

***

Joe and Mike were standing on a roadside bridge overlooking a park where a drug bust was about to go down. A detective and her informant were down in the parking area. They had been in position for over an hour in the blistering sun. They were passing the time discussing Joe's breakup.

"Ya know, maybe it's better to be single in this job," said Joe.

Mike snorted and nodded his head. "Maybe being married to the job is better."

They saw the informant get out of the detective's car. A late-model black vehicle pulled up alongside. Two people got out. The detective joined the informant for the transaction and then gave the sign for backup to move in. Joe and Mike launched themselves over the guardrail. The straggly plants they had thought were bushes were thin trees. They never considered the terrain going down the hill. They tumbled through branches, weeds, and briars. Hitting hard at the bottom, both were cut and scraped. Joe yelled, "Come on!"

Mike had dropped to his hands and knees. Now he was up and running toward the detective and her car.

By the time Mike and Joe ran up, the rest of the backup team had the two perpetrators handcuffed. "What in the hell happened to you two?" demanded the detective. "Good thing I didn't have to rely on you."

Mike, panting, looked at Joe. Joe had branches stuck in his hair, scrapes and bleeding cuts on his arms and hands, and a black eye already forming. Mike had fared much better, only suffering scratches and a cut lip. They were lucky. The detective didn't even write them up.

***

March 1, 1980 was an unusually frigid day in Columbus, with a temperature ranging from fifteen degrees high to a low of eight degrees. Mike was on the backup arrest team with three other undercover agents, *Ron, Larry, and Coop.* Ron had been pulled from the patrol division and loved tactical situations. Larry was the sergeant-in-charge. He had drawn up the tactical plan for this deal and had seniority in the unit. Coop had a deficit of poor eyesight, which was corrected with thick glasses. His assignment was to handle liquor violations in bars where the undercover officers worked. They were back up for a PCP buy (phencyclidine or Angel Dust, also called Angel Death). The informant, *Jimmy,* and *Deputy Tyler Smith* were in a four-door vehicle poised to meet the trafficker in an OSU stadium parking lot. The backup team was in a dark-colored van parked strategically away from streetlights.

Tyler had come on the force with Mike but was more experienced in this unit. Tyler was smart, and Mike felt he could depend on him to be ethical in his decisions. Everyone was on extra guard in case the trafficker was on PCP. PCP is a powerful hallucinatory substance and could cause a person to react aggressively. This drug scared Mike more than most because it made the addict unpredictable.

Tyler was to do the buy. He was in the passenger seat to expedite the transaction. Since it was dusk, it was dark enough for a cover but light enough to see the informant exit his car. His exit signaled to the police to make the arrest.

The officers were briefed the trafficker was in his twenties. At first, the officers thought he was an OSU student, but they learned later he just lived in the campus area.

The setup ran smoothly as an older model white Ford crusted with dirt arrived on time. The trafficker slipped into the backseat behind Tyler. Just a few moments before, the backup officers were whispering and teasing each other; now, the tenseness in the van was intoxicating. Just as planned, the informant opened his door and got out. The van with Mike, Ron, Larry, and Coop crawled closer to the unmarked car. Exiting on both sides, Mike and Ron were the first out. The car lit up. Gunshot. The car was rocking. Mike scuttled quickly up to the passenger back door side. He witnessed more flashes and heard more bursts of a gun. Crouching low with his gun out, Mike glanced to see Coop by the back wheel to his left. He nodded to him. Pausing, he counted to three and pulled on the car's handle. The handle gave, but the door didn't open. Jammed? Frozen? Mike motioned to Coop to meet him on the other side. Both ran low behind the car to the other side. The car was still rocking. Ron, already in position, waited for them to join him. Mike and Ron jerked both the front and the back doors on the driver's side. They could see the trafficker wrestling with Tyler over the seat. Mike saw blood smeared on Tyler's forehead. Sounds of shouting were a mash of curses and orders. Mike saw a small handgun on the back seat. Knocking it to the floor, Mike grabbed for the trafficker. Ron grabbed Tyler, yelling for him to let go of the trafficker. "We got him! It's okay!"

"He's got a gun!"

"Mike and Ron have him! Mike, got the gun?"

"It's on the floor."

"Grab his arms!"

"Call a squad! The guy's hit."

"What about Tyler!"

"He's good."

The trafficker was twisting and yelling. Screaming, he was shot. Mike and Coop pulled the 150-pound, wiry now suspect out of the car. He was still fighting, swinging at the officers. Both officers were aware of his blood soaking through his clothes. Ron and Larry joined them. The rusty smell of blood filled the car. As the suspect fought, blood smeared on all the officers' jackets and hands. Mike, holding onto the arms of the suspect, saw one of the officer's 45 as it arched up and struck the suspect on the back of the head. He felt the impact of the hit, but it didn't affect the perp. They finally succeeded in stretching the suspect across the trunk of the informant's car.

Yelling over the incoming ambulance siren, panting, Ron asked, "Anyone hit?"

The suspect had stopped fighting, but all the officers were still gripping him. They all shook their heads no. All the men were panting, floating vapor surrounding them. Some were even sweating from fighting the suspect.

Two EMTs came rushing up. Mike let go of the suspect. "He's suspected of having multiple gunshot wounds and possible ingested PCP," he yelled.

One EMT left to help a third with the gurney.

After helping two EMTs hold the suspect and strap him to the gurney, Ron accompanied the suspect to the hospital. The suspect had sustained five gunshots. One in his stomach. One in his wrist probably caused him to drop his gun, a few to his legs, and one to his privates.

Tyler was over to the side of the squad, dry heaving. EMTs had checked him out, saying he had a cut on his head. The slice wasn't so bad but would need stitches. The heaving was probably from fear and shock of the experience. Mike and the remaining officers helped Tyler into the van and took him to

The Ohio State Medical Center. They also dispatched a car to give his wife a ride to the hospital to be with him.

As they rode to the hospital, Tyler related what had happened. The informant had made an excuse to get out of the car as planned. Tyler made the purchase and secured the five grams of PCP, placing it in his pocket. Tyler reached for his gun in his ankle holster, pointed it over the seat back at the suspect, and said, "Police, you're under arrest."

When the suspect pulled out his small gun and brought it up to shoot, Tyler shot him in the stomach. As expected, the suspect folded over but lurched up again, pointing his gun. Tyler reported his face was contorted with anger. Tyler then emptied his 38. Five hit the suspect. The shot that hit his wrist made him drop his weapon.

The suspect recovered from his wounds and went to trial. He was convicted of trafficking and went to prison.

Tyler was off work for several months. His physical wound would heal quickly. But it took much more time for him to recover from the psychological pain of anxiety, nerves, and fear. Tyler returned for one more buy to prove he could overcome his fears. Mike and Tyler worked to pick up a dealer selling quaaludes. The buy was successful, but Tyler requested to be transferred to another division.

Strip Club and Bars

Brad Simpson was a railroad employee. He had to always carry equipment in his car because he claimed he was on a twenty-four hour call seven days a week. This was Mike's persona as he was assigned to visit nightclubs and nude strip clubs to purchase drugs. Cocaine was a big drug in the late 70s and early 80s, and it was his job to see how they could reduce the sale on the streets.

Mike would check into several strip clubs to start until he could be considered a regular. Most of them looked and smelled the same. The Columbus Health Department kept them relatively clean. Some had stages in the front with runways decorated with poles. Some had individual tables on either side of the runway with an aisle separating the customers from the stage. Others had seats and small tables up close. The clubs were hazed with cigarette smoke.

At one place, Mike became acquainted with Dena. Dena was almost past her prime as a dancer. In the clouded light of the strip club, Dena was tall, buxom, thin, and pleasant to admire. Up close, a patron could see the toll that life had taken on her. Her makeup was thick covering scars from acne as a kid. She was relying on bright shadows and long fake lashes to hide the lines around her eyes. Her hair was blonde, but during the times Mike would know her, she would change it several times.

Part of Mike's story as Brad was, he sometimes liked to get high when he was working. To supplement her dancing tips and salary, Dena sold drugs. She offered to get him LSD, so he ended up purchasing acid from her. The establishment proved to be a profitable spot because he bought several other types of drugs from other employees four to five times. Not really interested in these sellers, Mike wanted to find the suppliers. Dena would tell him about her childhood and gossip about several people who worked at the club. It became a regular thing that if Mike came into the club, Dena would sit with him after her set.

Besides his assignments, Mike proposed to his superiors to write a comprehensive training program for future undercover policemen. The lack of training Mike experienced when he started and the mistakes and dangers he had observed since joining the team haunted him. His proposal was accepted. During the day, Mike was training other officers not only in Central Ohio but around the state in a two-week course in basic undercover work.

During a class, a call came through Mike's undercover line. Dena said it was urgent that she talk to him and ask him a question. In a discussion with his superiors, they decided this was nothing to be overly concerned about. Feeling Dena herself was harmless, Mike still felt his guard needed to be up.

Mike went down to the strip club within the next week. After her set, Dena came and sat down with "Brad." "You look good. Have you been working outside?" Dena started the conversation light.

"Yeah, we had a major job on a Hamilton Road crossing."

"Is that what was causing all the traffic jams?

Mike said, "Yeah, we saw more than our share of middle fingers this week."

Dena laughed. "Brad, I'm glad you came. I need to ask you..." She leaned forward. "I heard you're an undercover cop."

Mike looked at her in confusion. He leaned forward to hear her as she whispered her comment, but now he sat back and laughed. "Where did ya hear that? Nah, I told you I work for CSX."

Dena was studying him. "We have our ways, Brad."

She laughed as he shook his head back and forth and said, "Nope, not me."

Leaning forward again so she was heard over the blaring music, she said, "Another barmaid, Charlie knows, said you're an undercover cop."

Mike had bent forward to hear her again. Leaning back in the chair again, he crossed his arms and reached his hand to rub his stubbly chin. "No way."

Dena looked at Mike coyly. "Nah, I trust you. Maybe it's just somebody who was jealous here at the club."

"Okay, maybe," Mike said. He took out his wallet and paid for the PCP she had gotten for him.

Not inclined to take the risk of being burned, Mike handed over that club to another detective.

Dena was eventually picked up and charged with felonies for drug trafficking. In a case like Dena, she agreed to work as an informant for the prosecutor to work off some time or lower her felony charges. Mike vouched for her. Her assignment was to go with him to other locations and introduce him to her suppliers.

During the interview that occurred after her arrest, Mike asked Dena, who identified him as an undercover. The barmaid Charlie was dating a deputy sheriff. This deputy was also in the Undercover Unit. He knew Mike. The deputy would check in on Charlie occasionally "to make sure everything was okay." What he was doing was making sure Charlie wasn't taking part in any illegal trafficking. He saw Mike go through the parking lot one night to his car. He warned Charlie that "Brad" was an undercover officer burning Mike in warning her off. Of course, that's when Charlie mentioned it to Dena.

Soon Charlie was arrested for a lower degree felony of trafficking and the deputy was offered a chance to resign, which he did.

***

The sheriff's department and the state liquor agency would team to work several cases at a time. In his rotation, Mike went into a bar with predominantly African American clientele. One of his contacts had mentioned he could make important connections there. His primary aim here was to buy pharmaceutical drugs from *Cha'relle*, a local young female.

One tall patron of the bar sat with Brad and Cha'relle. "Why *Dom*, how's Daisy?"

"She's good, Cha'relle. Good." Dom turned to Mike and

said, "Why're you here? There's a place for you just down the street. Why don't you go down there?"

Mike smiled at him. "I kinda walked in here and liked the company."

Cha'relle reached out and held Mike's arm. "Brad, don't pay any attention to Dom. We dated, but now he's with someone else. Turning her head to Dom, she said, "Go mind your own business."

Dom glared at her while he took his time rising from the chair. He joined some other guys at the bar. Talking with the other men, he kept turning to glower at the couple.

"Hey, white man. What the fuck are you doing in here?" One guy from the bar yelled at Mike.

"*Zion*, you hush up." Cha'relle yelled back.

"Cha'relle, I'm going to go."

"But we were just getting started."

"I'll come back another time."

He smiled at her, finished his beer, and sauntered out of the bar.

Mike called the state liquor agency, and they assigned an African American agent, *Christian*, who could back him up when Mike would visit this bar.

When he next visited this bar on his rotation, Christian was already there. Christian had found out Zion was Cha'relle's brother, and he threatened "to let the air of Mike's chest the next time he visited." He didn't like Mike messing with his sister. He thought Mike was taking advantage of her. Christian told Zion, "Relax. I'll take care it for you."

Christian approached Mike and Cha'relle at a table. Mike was wearing a Buckeye cap, so it was easy to drum up a conversation about the Buckeye's next season. The conversation led to the upcoming weekend and progressed to Mike saying he was looking for weed. Christian mentioned he had some for him. They went outside to transact "the deal." As they were ten feet from the front door, both Mike and Christian noticed Zion leaving, scanning the parking lot as he walked. They kept walking to Christian's car to complete "the transaction." They watched as Zion leaned against a car, lit a cigarette, and played with his blade.

The bar was reassigned to another member of the team.

PART TWO

Michael

The Cartel

Washington Courthouse 1980

Mike was working Special Duty at The Ohio State football games. After a game, Captain Ron Hellman, his supervisor, pulled Mike aside.

"Mike, Sheriff McDonald of Fayette County is interested in you doing some undercover work in his community. There are several complaints from citizens concerning drug trafficking. Would you be interested in going down starting in October and seeing what you can find out?"

"I'd love to. I think it's time for me to get out of the Columbus area for a bit."

Mike was involved in quite a few drug investigations as of late, and his look was getting to be too well-known. He needed to let things cool down a bit.

In October 1980, Washington Courthouse was the county seat of Fayette County. The population was just over twelve thousand. A place where everybody knows everybody. For an undercover and a new face, a small community can be a challenging place to work. It's even harder if there isn't a confidante or informant that could introduce that undercover around to members of the community that are involved in drug trafficking.

The first few times Mike went to the town, he took *Evan*, an off-duty officer who wanted to get a taste of undercover work. Mike felt he needed backup since he was unknown to the people in the area.

The two men started hitting several bars. People were not friendly. It was understandable. Most folks felt a new face was a liquor agent or a narcotics officer.

Mike tried the alternative approach. They would go down early, about four or five o'clock, and get to know the bartenders. If the bartender would get to know him and like him, he may be considered okay.

Mike introduced himself as Jimmy and said that he worked for the railroad. It would explain his not living there, and his comings and goings. Mike told people he met he suspected he may be hot in the Columbus area with warrants out for his arrest. In Washington Courthouse, he thought he'd be safe.

Days grew to weeks. Weeks grew to a month. Mike didn't connect to any drug transactions.

Mike then remembered Dena. Dena, a stripper, was an informant who Mike had helped arrest for selling LSD, PCP, and weed. Part of her agreement to lower the time of her sentencing was she would cooperate and introduce Mike to the drug dealers who had supplied her. Mike's recollection was that Dena knew some people down in Washington Courthouse.

Mike met with Dena and asked her if she would go down with him and his partner, Evan, and introduce them around. She agreed.

Dena sashayed into the first bar and immediately and loudly announced her return. *Mick*, the bartender who had been friendly but not willing to talk much to Mike, greeted her with "God, girl, where have you been?"

Dena replied, posing with her hand on her hip, "Well, Mick, you know I'm in demand!"

After chatting a bit, Dena asked Mick where a few of her old friends were and if they were still coming into the bar. They were. She ordered a vodka and soda and told Mick to put it on Jimmy's (Mike's) tab.

Putting her arm around Mike's shoulders, she said, "You know, Jimmy, don't you?"

Mick, still leery, said, "How'd you two meet?"

"Where do you think? He comes and sees me dance. We were talking, and he said he likes coming down here and invited me to join him and Evan. Evan, you have to come and see me dance, too."

Evan grinned and said, "Absolutely, that's all Jimmy talks about is how you can dance."

They took her down four times before Mike could make a connection and purchase a small amount of marijuana. After proving he was okay to Mick through knowing Dena, Mike continued his visits to the bar now by himself. Mike bought some Quaaludes (panty droppers), Xanax, Sopors, and Lemon 714s.

The Washington Courthouse police chief and Fayette County sheriff identified people who they knew were trafficking in drugs but couldn't prove it. On the list, they said there were some folks that were dangerous, and they wanted Mike to be aware. One of the "folks" on the list was *Kyle Safford*. Kyle was currently in prison for shooting a guy.

Sitting at the bar one night, Mike met *Rena Preston*.

"Jimmy, whatcha doing down here?"

"I like it here. I work for the railroad."

"Engineer?" Laughing, she pretended to pull a horn.

"Nah. I'm a carman."

Playing with her hair, Rena leaned on the bar flirting. "Exactly what does a carman do?"

"Mostly make sure everything on the cars or locomotives work. Test parts, replace parts, check for safety." Mike shrugged. "Pays the bills."

"Now, how does a carman have fun?"

"I party, you know." Mike smiled, then turned to sip his beer.

Rena was a regular at the bar. She was a pretty woman with long, dark hair and doe-like eyes. She was pleasant to be with and had an infectious laugh. Telling Mike her story, she married early and was now divorced with two children. Her mom watched her kids so she could have a break.

He learned she worked as a clerk for a local company. She mentioned it was hard sometimes to make ends meet. But she had learned how to manage. He commiserated with her and told her he would move drugs in the Columbus area to help pay his bills.

"My brother Kyle used to help me out, but he's in prison now. His time is almost up, so things should be better."

"I'd like to meet him. I did some time up in Toledo."

"You did? What for?"

"Theft. I was young and stupid. Shoulda known better."

Mike asked the last name of her brother. Until then, Mike hadn't realized her connection to the man the police chief and sheriff had mentioned to him.

As soon as Mike returned to the office and finished his reports, he researched Kyle's name. Kyle had been a frequent resident of prison.

Mike met with officers of Washington Courthouse to receive money to buy drugs. He informed the officials that he had met Rena and that Kyle was about to be freed from prison. They all knew Kyle would go right back into the trafficking business as soon as he was released. Rena had stated Kyle intended to be very careful who he sold to, so he didn't go back to prison again.

Mike was excited. When he discussed Kyle with his supervisor, he was warned several times Kyle was dangerous.

During the time Mike was meeting with these officials, Rena introduced him to the three *Brubeck* brothers. Constantly fighting and verbally abusive to each other and other people, all three were twenty-something and worked various labor jobs. They were also into selling small amounts of marijuana, pills, and cocaine. Mike mentioned to the Brubecks that he was interested in working with them and making some extra cash. When they talked about purchasing LSD, they offered to introduce him to *Ailene Holtermans*. They thought she could get 10 to 15 hits for them.

Holtermans was a massive thorn in the side of local law enforcement. Middle-aged, physically, and emotionally wiry, they couldn't get near her. She, by reputation, was violent.

Two of the Brubecks took Mike to Holtermans's house. Mike was surprised when they pulled up in front of it. Her house was a manicured white two-story federalist-style structure. A muscular, military-statured man greeted them at the front door. As he led them to a small sitting room, Mike glimpsed at the dining room. He was impressed with the formal antique dining room suite. The sitting room was furnished sparsely with a green couch, a coffee table, and a straight-backed chair. The greeter slid the wood doors shut behind him. Mike and the Brubecks stood waiting to make their purchase. The doors slid open, and Ailene Holtermans entered the room. Her graying hair was shoulder length, and she was tall. It was Mike she immediately scrutinized as she came into the room, looking him up and down. Her elongated face had little make-up except for her eyes. Her black eyeliner accented the steel gray coldness of her stare. Mike felt exposed. He was a thirty-something guy with the twenty-something Brubecks - an unknown face. He knew Holtermans was going to be an issue for him.

"Who are you?"

"Jimmy Williams."

"Where do you work?"

"Conrail, Columbus and Ohio River Railroad."

"Let me see your driver's license."

Mike's license matched his undercover identity. It had a legitimate street name but a bogus number. She told them all to sit on the couch while she sat in the chair. Lying on the coffee table was a sandwich bag of marijuana in an ashtray. She reached into her pocket and took out a pack of cigarettes. While she stared at Mike, she took one out. Placing the pack back in her pocket, she took out a lighter and lit the cigarette. All deliberate, while keeping her eyes on Mike.

Mike, trying to act naturally under her glare, leaned forward, clenching his hands between his legs, his elbows on his knees. "What are you going to do with the LSD?" she asked as she exhaled smoke.

"Sell it."

It dawned on Mike that she may want him to smoke a joint or take a drug. He knew how he reacted to any of her questions or demands would be determine how this situation would turn out. He didn't have a gun on him, and he was relatively positive there was one in the house.

"Look, if you don't trust me, I can leave."

Both Brubecks shifted when he said this.

"If you don't want my money, no sweat."

"I think you're a cop."

Though her posture in the chair didn't show her nervousness; her hand holding the cigarette was shaky. "Fuck it. I'm not taking a chance. I'm not giving you shit. I'm not giving you anything. I'm not going to hand you anything. I'm going to leave this room. If you have money, you can lay it down on the table, or you can give it to Pat Brabeck." Nodding at him as she said this.

She left the room. Mike laid the fifty dollars on the table. Neither one of the Brubecks touched it. They had discussed buying 15 hits of LSD, about three or four dollars apiece.

Shortly, she came back into the room and told Mike to turn his back. The hair on the back of his neck raised, not knowing if she had returned with a gun.

Devil's Disciples

When Holtermans said Mike could turn around, he kept his eyes on her as he picked up a cellophane wrapper containing microdots of LSD from the table. He placed the wrapper in his front pants pocket almost in slow motion. He suspected she had scooped up the money and placed the cellophane wrapper on the table while he was turned around. He still wasn't sure if she was hiding a gun.

Mike knew she was trying to isolate herself to avoid trouble in case he was a police officer.

As they left, Holtermans said, "No offense, but I don't want to work with someone I don't know. From now on, you'll have to give your money to one of those guys if you want any more product. They can pick it up or whatever. I just don't want just anybody coming to my place."

That was the last transaction Mike had in her residence. He bought more from the Brubecks, who purchased his order from her. He realized there was a lot of acid being sold in Washington Courthouse.

"Jimmy" (Mike) was making a name for himself as a trafficker. In December, Mike was buying from many individuals. He was purchasing Quaaludes, LSD, marijuana, Sopors, and small amounts of cocaine. His enterprise would take him to other counties.

Visiting the Washington Courthouse bar, Rena said her brother was out of the penitentiary and would like to meet him.

On parole, Kyle was being very cautious. If he had any violations, he would go back to any time he had "on the shelf." Because he was too well-known to law enforcement, he couldn't meet in the bar. He would be recognized and charged with a parole violation. Mike was cautious about where they would meet since Kyle was reportedly violent. He was not only incarcerated for his crime, but he also aggressively resisted arrest. After Rena told Mike that Kyle had serious connections for drugs, he expressed his hope that Kyle would work with him. He would like to collaborate to purchase large amounts of drugs to resell.

Rena vouched for Mike to Kyle. Kyle was willing if Mike was 'cool.' 'Cool' to law enforcement was the officer had to be patient and prepared to meet the target.

During the discussion about a meeting, Rena told Mike, "Kyle is staying with my parents right now. Finding a private meeting place near my parents' house is a problem. Kyle lost his driver's license. It was revoked before he went to jail. I lost mine too, for different reasons."

"Fine. I can take my car just to talk."

Mike met them one evening midweek. He pulled up to Safford's parents' residence, and Kyle came out of the house. Rena was already in the front seat. Kyle climbed into the back seat behind Rena. Though Mike was cautious about Kyle, he at least felt in control since he was driving.

They stopped in a nearby park and sat in a small picnic shelter with an open stone fireplace. Mike and Kyle shook hands as they sat across from each other at a table. Mike sized him up to be about average build. Kyle's thick glasses made his beady, small eyes look droopy and magnified.

After talking for a while, Mike knew Kyle wasn't dumb. He knew the street and the ins and outs of the drug world. He had been in and out of prison several times for trafficking.

"Rena says she's known you for a while. She said you're up from around Columbus, and you've got connections in Toledo."

"Yeah. I spent some time in jail." Mike didn't want to share he was in prison because Kyle might know some things about prison, he might not be aware of. Since Mike began his career working in the Franklin County jail, he felt more comfortable referring to jail. He knew the atmosphere and what you could or could not do.

Kyle seemed to respect that. "I understand you want to make some money."

"Yeah."

"Well, I can get you some acid."

"Oh really. What kind of price?"

"It depends on what you're buying. The more you buy, the cheaper it goes."

Mike knew it was dangerous to buy small quantities of street dope. The source expects you're buying it for personal use and that you would use it in front of them.

"I don't know what you're talking about large amounts. Fifteen to twenty hits. I don't make any money that way."

"We can get a hundred, you know? If you got the money, maybe eventually a thousand."

"Maybe what we can do is start with a hundred hits. Depending on the price, kind of go from there. If it goes good, we can go for more."

"Pretty cool. I can do that. I have to make a connection down in Pickaway County in Circleville. My friend's a biker in the Devil's Disciples."

Mike's nerves clinched. He knew a person has to pay his dues to even go into a clubhouse. All Kyle saw was Mike's eyebrows raised as if he was impressed. Police consider motorcyclists extremely dangerous. They are aggressive and violent.

Kyle said, "If you can come down on a Saturday, I'd be willing to make that connection for you. They don't really have a phone in the trailer we're going to. It's in the boonies. I'll go before we go down and talk to my connect. I'll order one hundred hits, and we'll see what it will be."

Mike nodded. "Fine, let's set it up at a time on Saturday."

"4:30'll do."

Mike didn't want to wear a wire. Depending on the situation, who's there, and what goes on, he knew there was a strong possibility the bikers would pat him down. He didn't want to take a partner. Since Kyle hadn't met a partner, it could screw things up. He contacted surveillance and let them know roughly where he would be located. He advised they could follow, but they couldn't be close. Kyle could not be spooked. Kyle might even have a counter-surveillance set up. Mike decided not to even take a gun. He felt that if Kyle took him into the bikers' place and was patted down, the gang would just take the gun. Potentially, that would cause more problems. It could also result in questions.

Mike was edgy when he picked Kyle up on Saturday. Kyle was a high-energy person, always moving, never laid back. Kyle was known to do a lot of LSD and wore dark glasses, so it was hard to tell if his eyes were dilated. Mike knew Kyle carried a small gun in his pocket or in the back of his pants. Mike was concerned about his judgment if he was on acid when they were together. Something dangerous could occur.

They headed out to Laurelville, Ohio. The closest landmark to Laurelville was Tar Hallow State Park and Wayne National Forest. According to the 2010 census, over five hundred people lived in the village. In the foothills of the Appalachians, the area was remote. They traveled the back roads. After about an hour, they turned onto a gravel road. The crunching and bumpy ride ended at a dilapidated, rusted trailer. Four large motorcycles were parked outside, along with a couple of cars and an old pickup truck. Mike could feel his nerves creep up his spine.

"Kyle, you can go inside. I can wait out here. Or whatever."

"No, come on, Jimmy. They ain't gonna do anything. They want you to see 'em, you know?"

Mike got out of the car reluctantly. Kyle bounded up the rickety lopsided stair and opened the squealing door. Mike half expected the door handle to come out in Kyle's hand. The stair seemed solid enough as he put his weight on it, but he swore he could feel the trailer list as he went in.

As his eyes adjusted, he could see five males, all seated, watching a rabbit-eared television. On the television stand rested a .45-caliber handgun. Mike knew the gun was there to let him know they were armed. All Mike could think of was: *Do I look like a cop? Do I smell like a cop? Do I walk like a cop?* The odor of weed permeated the trailer.

Kyle introduced Mike to *Gene*. Mike extended his hand. Gene looked at it, laughed, and absorbed Mike's hand in an iron grip. Mike felt like he was in a movie. The guy looked like a stereotypical biker, with shoulder-length, dark hair, a stubbled face, and wearing a red handkerchief headband. Instead of a leather vest, Gene wore a flannel shirt and jeans. All five men looked like that, with a few modifications and added tats that could be seen peeking from rolled-up sleeves.

Mike noticed that one guy close to him was passing around a joint. He wondered if he was going to have to fake smoking. They first offered the joint to Kyle.

"No thanks, I can't in case I have to 'drop urine.'"

He then offered it to Mike. "No, I'm driving."

The pressure disappeared. Mike was thankful.

Addressing his question to Mike, Gene asked, "So, how much do you want?"

Kyle answered, "He wants a hundred."

Gene got up and walked to the kitchen area. Mike watched as he took out a small container and a pill-counter tray. Gene dumped a shower of microdots onto the tray. He took a stiletto knife from his boot to count the microdots until he reached one hundred. He placed all of them into a plastic sandwich bag and handed it to Kyle. Kyle gave it to Mike.

Mike reached into the front pocket of his worn jeans and counted out a bunch of twenties and one ten. He gave the money to Kyle, and Kyle gave it to Gene.

"Thanks, guys. I appreciate it. If I can get rid of these and make some money, I'd like to do more."

Gene nodded. "Sure, we do five hundred or a thousand. If you've got the money, we can rock and roll with you."

Mike was glad to get back into the car. Kyle climbed into the passenger side.

"Dude, what do I owe you?"

"Twenty bucks. And how about a couple of hits?"

Mike didn't want to do that. First, he'd need special permission. It meant he would do a transaction, buying and selling. The only way he could do it is if it would put his undercover identity at risk.

"There's only a hundred here, dude. Why don't I give you a few bucks, then you can buy a few hits yourself?"

Mike gave Kyle twenty-five dollars for doing the deal for him. "Here's ten more. Go for it if you want to pick some more up from Gene."

Kyle took the money and went back inside. He came back out after about five or six minutes. Once inside the car, he took out three hits and put them in his mouth under his tongue.

Mike couldn't believe it. Driving back to Kyle's place would be about forty-five minutes. Kyle could hallucinate, start flaying around... anything could happen.

The Round up

Mike attempted to get back to Kyle's house as quickly as possible, rolling through an occasional stop sign, being careful but going over the speed limit. At one point, Kyle started flinching. He would take his right hand and swipe at the windshield.

"Are you seeing something?"

"Yeah, bugs."

Mike kept thinking about the gun in Kyle's pocket and kept looking for a place to pull over… if he had to.

Thirty-five minutes later, with Kyle still swiping and ducking at imaginary bugs, Mike pulled in front of Kyle's place. Mike gave Kyle one hundred dollars for taking him out to Laurelville, and so Kyle could make some money. Mike was exhausted from watching the road and Kyle, but he traveled back to the office and met with the surveillance team to debrief.

Mike made a few more transactions, bringing Kyle along as a go-between. Finally, Kyle told Mike that Gene was feeling pressure from the county and didn't think it was a good idea for Kyle to keep bringing Mike. Mike knew the real reason was Kyle was afraid Mike would cut him out of the transactions.

Mike, Kyle, and Rena would see a lot of each other in the coming months. Mike would tell them he was thinking of moving to Florida because a buddy of his wanted him to move down there. Soon Rena and Kyle would say they were thinking of moving down there with him. They thought the move would allow them to start over. Mike believed the ploy would allow him save hundreds of man-hours in keeping track of them. Mike set it up that they all would leave on February fourteen. As they were packing and celebrating, Mike was working to organize a giant sweep.

Earlier in the month, Mike, with the help of Fayette County Prosecutor Hank Rosman, had hidden in a car on his way to the Washington County Courthouse to testify to a Grand Jury. Law enforcement agencies came together to write indictments which would allow officers to arrest forty-seven people in a three-county area. They were about to enforce two hundred counts of drug trafficking.

On Valentine's Day, 1981, Mike went down to an old elementary education school in Madison Mills. He would be greeted by the sight of the cruisers of one hundred law enforcement officers representing county sheriffs, city police, and state liquor agents. Mike, at 29, instructed over one hundred officers from all over the state on what he had uncovered, what areas to be wary of, and who might be the most violent of the individuals to arrest, including Kyle and the members of the motorcycle gang, Devil's Disciples. He also had to instruct them on the plan for the sweep. They were all to wait and descend on their targets simultaneously. Fourteen search warrants were going to be executed for liquor violations and drug deals. Ironically, some individuals they were looking for that night would be in those served establishments, including Kyle and Rena.

Darkness falls early in Ohio winters. Mike watched the mile-long bright red, pulsing lights as the cruisers pulled out and sped down Route 62. The raid was successful and reports of it hit all the major news outlets in the State of Ohio. That day, the raids reaped five hundred hits of LSD from the bikers in Laurelville alone.

Mike, after each transaction, had returned to the sheriff's office and made meticulous notes. He wrote out what people were wearing, what hand they gave him the drugs, and notes on the various bills he paid with. He made sure each perpetrator had at least three counts against them, so deals could be made at the time of prosecution.

Defense attorneys looked at any small chink that they could. The defendants were angry that Jimmy, their friend, or buyer, was really Mike, an undercover cop. Seven defendants went to trial. Seven convictions were obtained. A domino effect would occur with individuals charged and pleading out from that point. Rena Safford would plead guilty and receive no help since she refused to testify against her brother.

Kyle Safford was the one person who fought the indictments. Kyle had eight counts of aggravated trafficking against him. His charges covered two counties. He faced a mandatory seven to twenty-five years in prison. Mike and the prosecutor believed since he had a previous record, he would do more than the minimum of seven years.

Mike paced and hardly slept the night before the trial for Kyle Safford. He had to be well-prepared for all the trials knowing the defense attorneys would go after each summary, how he did his undercover work, and how he was trained. But for Safford, that attorney would question each tiny detail of each transaction Mike and Kyle made. For Mike, the environment of the courtroom was nerve-wracking. He could feel Kyle's eyes on him, wanting to destroy him, his reputation, and work. Since Mike had memorized his reports, each transaction, the dates, times, and everything they had done, he didn't use any notes on the witness stand. He could see Kyle's eyes, enlarged by his thick glasses, glaring at him. Once he laid his hand on the Bible, Mike would answer questions while looking at the jury, the attorneys, and the judge.

The trial took three days. The jury came back and convicted Kyle of all charges. As an officer led Kyle out, he kept his eyes on Mike. Mike felt that if there were any individuals in his career, he would fear getting out of prison and come looking for him - it would be Kyle Safford.

PART THREE

Michael mid-1980s

Marielitos

The Caravan

Marielitos were the Cuban immigrants who left Cuba from the Port of Mariel, starting in April 1980. According to NPR's *Talk of the Nation*, "Marielitos' Stories, 30 Years After the Boatlift," "Cuban leader Fidel Castro declared the Port of Mariel open, permitting Cubans to freely depart to the U.S." From April to September, approximately 125,000 Cubans arrived in the Mariel Boatlift. Most immigrants were families, but the boatlift "became synonymous with criminals, prisoners, and the mentally ill."

The Catholic Church placed many of the Cuban in parts of the country to help assimilate them into the United States. The church relocated several individuals to the Columbus area.

Mike and his partner, *Mark Atman*, worked together for twenty years. Mike was gregarious; Mark laid back. They read each other's signals without fail. They planned their moves on cases together. In possible dangerous situations, they would prepare mentally by saying a prayer for each other.

Informants let them know there was quite a bit of cocaine sold by Cubans in the Short North area of Columbus. A couple of girls, known prostitutes associated with the Cubans, had stolen some cocaine. The girls were shot and dumped in a stream. The girls were last seen in this Short North area. Mike and his partner knew that because the girls were prostitutes, not much effort would be spent solving the case. They recognized the prevailing attitude about prostitutes and people who, like these two girls, were struggling with substance abuse. Not that they didn't respect the Homicide

Department of the Columbus Police Department or other detectives of the Franklin County Sheriff's Department. Nor did they criticize either department; they were too professional. The traditional view was people who were drug and substance users should go out and get a job like everyone else. Most people did not realize then that addiction changes brain chemistry. Choices diminished as drug and substance abuse increased.

Mike and Mark went undercover in the Short North area to see if they could find out more about the drug situation and possibly turn up information about the murders. Mike took the undercover name, Eddie. Mark became Phil. Eddie wore earrings that gave the impression he was into drugs. Wanting to make a statement, he wore a skull stud or a tiny dangling spoon; both were popular in the mid80s with the cocaine crowd. He wore a gold nugget that hung loosely on a gold chain as a conversation piece. Phil also wore jewelry in the same vein, but more subdued.

Working with a keen confidential source named *Charlene* since the early 1980s, they had a generous amount of intelligence to work with. Charlene had worked in many strip and go-go joints throughout central Ohio. She knew many of the young prostitutes and about the drug activity in the Short North area. Knowing she knew some of the Cuban individuals who were known traffickers of large amounts of cocaine, the officers took the intel from her and worked to develop probable cause for arrest or search warrants to execute. Charlene became their ear on the street. If she heard anyone talking about the two guys named Eddie and Phil being narcotic cops, she let them know. None of the officers knew Charlene's reasons for working with them. Rumors were she had lost someone to drugs, but no one was certain, and Charlene would shrug off their questions.

Mike and Mark started in a bar called The Caravan on Fourth Avenue and High Street where the Cubans and prostitutes hung out. The plan was to start early in the evening, around five o'clock, so they could get to know the bartenders. They would pass themselves off as construction workers just getting off work.

Initially, Mike and Mark walked into The Caravan and ordered a beer. One of them got up and looked at the jukebox to learn what type of music was popular there. They chose a song like "Cocaine" by Eric Clapton that sent a message in hopes it would start a conversation. They made sure it would play several times. After a while, when they entered The Caravan, the bartender greeted them. They discussed their jobs, complained about their fictitious supervisors, and told stories about each other.

One late afternoon, Mike and Mark were in the bar, and Mike thought a guy looked familiar at the end of the bar. As he and Mark talked, the guy kept looking at Mike. At one point, Mike stood and went over to the jukebox to play "Cocaine," and the man followed him with his eyes. Suddenly, Mike figured it out. The guy had bought dope from him a couple of years ago, and he had sent him to prison. He was a person who had accepted responsibility for his drug charges and had sat down with officers to cooperate with an investigation. As Mike recalled, it was a state case as opposed to a federal case.

Mike walked to the end of the bar as if he was going to go to the men's room. He stopped, turned, and leaned on the bar next to the man. The man looked at him. Looking straight ahead, Mike nodded. "How about we go into the men's room and talk?"

The guy started talking as soon as the door closed. "Look, I just got out of jail. I know who you are, and I don't want any problems." He raised his hands. "You're probably working. I'm not going to burn you or say anything to anyone." He gestured toward the exit to the men's room. "I promise you that. I will not do that to you."

Mike looked at him for a while, scanning his face as if he was reading him, then nodded. "Thanks."

Mike felt comfortable the man would keep his word.

He exited the men's room and returned to sit with Mark. Mike filled him in about the conversation since the bartender was serving people at the other end of the bar. Mark was paranoid that the guy could create issues that could burn them with the bartender. They decided to be cautious and use

Charlene. She could talk to the bartender and see if anything was said to him.

Ten minutes after the conversation with Mike, the guy who recognized him as a cop, left.

Charleen went in the next day and talked to the bartender and a few patrons. She didn't pick up any conversations about Eddie and Phil.

A few days after the incident, the bartender suggested they come in later when the bar activity picked up. They both agreed they would take him up on it.

A variety of people came into the bar. The clientele was ethnically diverse. Some were good people. Some were dangerous persons that had a history of burglaries, robberies, or drug trafficking.

A few nights later, Mike played "Cocaine" several times. He felt a man sit down on the barstool next to him. He turned to nod to him and saw two women standing behind him. Behind them was Charlene. Mike recognized him as *Sabino Terez*, one of the Cubans who had allegedly dealt cocaine.

"You like coca?"

Mike nodded. "I do like coca."

Sabino turned to one woman and said something to her in Spanish.

"He says he likes the gold nugget on your chain. He wants to know if you will take twenty-five dollars for it."

Turning his body to talk to them, Mike said, "I can't give it to him for that or any other amount of money. It's too special to me. It was my girlfriend's. She was in a bad car accident a while ago, spent a long time in the hospital, and died from her injuries. I took all the jewelry that I gave her and melted it down. It's all I have of her."

Sabino seemed to believe Mike's tale. The Marielitos were not yet schooled in a lot of the devices of the undercover officers and the country's laws, so they seemed naïve. Mike still had to be careful because the two girls with Sabino were aware of how the cops operated in the area. "I can't sell you this, but I like the coca," Mike said, gesturing to the gold nugget. Sabino offered to give Mike a quarter gram of cocaine for the nugget.

"No, I'm not trading cocaine or money for this nugget. But I am interested in getting a gram of cocaine."

The girl translated to Mike that Sabino had the cocaine with him. Mike could go out to the car with him to do the transaction.

"Okay, that's fine. But let's go to my car; it's parked just outside the bar."

He told Mark he'd be right back, that he was going outside to the car. Mark had no idea at that moment what was going down. Mike couldn't tell him. Sabino told the girls to stay in the bar.

When they arrived at Mike's car, Mike climbed into the driver's side, and Sabino on the passenger side. Sabino took out a small container. He had packed plastic baggies with a quarter gram or half a gram. "Twenty-five dollars," he said.

Mike gave him cash, a twenty-dollar and five-dollar bill. "Thanks. If I like this, I'd like to come back and get some more."

The Cuban smiled and said in a thick accent, "Okay, I take care of you."

Mike noted Sabino smoked cigarettes and drank beer. He now knew also he liked jewelry. The next day he went to the Sheriff's Department and Franklin County Prosecutor's office to gain permission to take unclaimed jewelry that was to be destroyed from the Property Room. Jewelry obtained from burglaries sometimes is ordered by the court to be destroyed when unclaimed by owners. After he received permission, Mike recorded each piece and took photos. The plan was to use the jewelry to purchase drugs on the street.

Mike's cover story was he had a guy who would commit a B and E (breaking and entering) or rob a jewelry store and then turn the property over to Eddie to sell. He also had a connection where he could obtain Coors© beer from the distributor. Since Coors© hadn't been approved in this area, it could not be sold. Sabino liked bottled beer, so Mike got cases to trade along with the jewelry. Mike and Mark would also arrange for racks of cigarettes like a person would see in a convenient store.

They put these racks in the back of their undercover car, went into the bar, and let everyone know they had these racks of cigarettes to sell. With permission from the prosecutor and the Sheriff's Department, they would take drugs in trade.

Short North Experiences

As the case went on, Mark and Mike met other local individuals trafficking pills, marijuana, and cocaine. They would also witness the prostitution that went on in the area. A john could get just about any service he wanted at The Caravan or in the parking lot. Mark and Mike were regularly seeing girls in and out, turning tricks.

Many girls were on stimulants like cocaine and downers like Xanax, Valium, Percocet, and Percodan. They lived with Cubans doing their errands, cooking their food, selling, or hooking a person up to buy drugs, turning tricks, translating for them, plus providing sex. In return, the Cubans would provide them with drugs.

One time in a transaction, one girl offered to help Mike purchase a fifty-dollar bag of cocaine. In return, she wanted a twenty-five-dollar bag for her trouble. Mike said fine, having received permission beforehand from the prosecutor and Sheriff's Department.

They left The Caravan and walked to a decrepit three-story apartment building on Buttles Avenue and High Street. Mike and his contact went up the creaking stairs. The stairwell smelled musty, and some of the paint was peeling away from the plaster. As they walked down the hall to access more stairs, Mike could see through open doors. The apartments were filthy and smelled of garbage. He could see debilitated people sprawled on mattresses or on the floor, drunk.

He and the girl finally reached the upper level. After seeing more of the same on this floor, they came to an apartment with a closed door. The girl knocked. Anticipating the door opening, Mike braced himself for what he would find. He could feel a surge of adrenalin.

Another female opened the door. She gestured for them to go inside. Mike swallowed the bile that rose in his throat from what he saw. This apartment was more significant and contained more worn, stained furniture than the ones he saw downstairs. Three Cubans and two white males were bending over a table with a mirror covered with stripes of powder cocaine. They took turns as they snorted the stuff. One of the three prostitutes in the room had liquified cocaine in a spoon. As if it was in slow motion, Mike saw her take a syringe and pull the liquid into the barrel of a needle. Another girl put her hands around the girl's arm to constrict her blood to make a vein pop up. The girl with the syringe then slid the tip into her own vein. He saw her press the plunger slowly until it met with the barrel top. He watched as she withdrew the tip and sighed.

Mike's contact laughed at his pallid face. He roused himself from the scene since he was dealing with street-level drugs; he had to be alert. The traffickers could expect him to use his purchased drugs in front of them. He felt the carotid artery in his neck pulsing. He needed to concentrate on getting the transaction done and get out of there.

His contact talked to one of the Cubans, *Elefante Fernandez*. The large man looked down at the girl and said, "What do you want?"

"A fifty-dollar bag and a twenty-five."

He handed her two bags. She turned to hand Mike the fifty-dollar bag and put the twenty-five-dollar bag in her purse. She gave Elefante the seventy-five dollars Mike had given her earlier. Fernandez barely looked at Mike.

They turned together and walked out of the apartment. Mike realized he was shaky as they headed down the stairs and came out of the building. He took a deep breath of night air to relax his nerves as he stood on the sidewalk. The girl walked ahead to go back to the Caravan.

Mike knew he wouldn't be able to recognize anyone in the apartment except Fernandez. The squalor and blatant nature of the drug use and the sense of danger around him hampered his view and observation skills.

Heading back to The Caravan, he met Mark, where they had agreed to meet after doing their separate transactions. In the mid-80s, the undercover officer could decide on their own as case agents if they needed backup, as long as they felt comfortable and safe in a situation.

Later, at their office, the officers exchanged their experiences. Mark had checked out what they thought was a trafficker's house and was almost caught by their own detectives. He had spotted them as they were exiting their vehicles and slipped out the back door and through an alley. Both Mark and Mike questioned why that door hadn't been covered.

***

A well-known person for anything from stolen property to trafficking drugs was *Edwin Nigleburger*. He also was known for taking any drugs he could get his hands on and was hardly ever sober. Nigleburger had been in an accident at one time and had a steel plate in his skull. He knew right from wrong, but it couldn't be said he could make complicated decisions. He had connections all over for all types of drugs. Mike and Mark tried to develop a relationship with him.

When Mike and Mark went to Nigleburger's dope house in the Short North for a transaction of cocaine, they went in the early hour of 3 A.M. They hoped that by going so early, most of the party people would be gone.

They knocked on the required back door. Nigleburger met them at the door wearing only his white jockey underwear. Sticking out of his left thigh was an Insulin 100 syringe. Mark coughed and looked down. Mike stepped back. Besides the syringe, Nigleburger had dried blood on the inside of his wrists and elbows.

After an uncomfortable pause, Mark said, "My God, what are you doing?"

Frustrated, Nigleburger responded, "I can't get a vein up, so I had to hit it in a muscle. Come on in."

Aware of how high and possibly aggressive Nigleburger could be, they were leery of entering the house. But they also did not want to offend him, so Mark and Mike stepped into the kitchen.

Mike looked around the kitchen to become aware of his surroundings. Dirty, crusted dishes were in the sink. On the stove, pots sat with food caked in them. As he stared at the greasy plates and pots, he swore he saw movement on them and the sink splashboards. There was no edible food anywhere. A couple of boxes of ten count insulin syringes were on a shelf across from the refrigerator. All unopened. Scattered on the counters and a small table were small saucers with needles.

While Nigleburger went upstairs to fill their order, Mike and Mark moved into the tiny living room. Mike recognized five locals, all in some stage of preparing to use or trade a needle. A Kentucky Fried Chicken tub sat on a coffee table centralized between the few seats. Peering in the tub, Mike saw water with a tinge of pink. He motioned for Mark to look. He looked in the bucket and grimaced.

They watched as several passed a syringe around. Whoever had it would stick the tip into the pink water of the tub and draw the water into the barrel. Pressing the plunger, the person would squirt the water back into the container. The following person would then fill it with liquid cocaine from a spoon and use the syringe.

A young woman came into the room, tapping her arm, trying to find a vein. Mike recalled her to be a local prostitute. When the tapping didn't work on either arm, she stood, unbuttoned, and zipped down her jeans, and dropped them to her ankles. One guy noticed her and told her to go into the other room. She registered disgust at the comment, gathered her things, stepped out of her jeans, and walked bottomless back into the other room.

Mark nodded to Mike. He recognized *Roger*, another local guy, who he knew to be heavily into stimulants. Roger perceived Mark and Mike as guys from the Caravan who fenced a lot of items. Roger was quick to acknowledge them. When Roger's turn came to use the syringe, he scooped the cocaine from a bag with a spoon. Heating it until it was liquid, he elaborately took a cotton swab from his pocket and dabbed it into the pinkish mixture. Sticking the tip into the cotton as a filter to block impurities, he drew the cocaine into the barrel and looked at Mark and Mike. "Watch," he said.

Using his left hand, he stuck the tip of the needle into the top of his right hand. He watched Mark and Mike's reactions.

His eyes were wide, and his pupils were dilated from stimulants. Teeth gritted; he pressed the plunger. He pulled the tip out of his hand and said, "Wow, good cocaine. Let me show you what a real man can do."

With his right hand still dripping blood from his injection, he put the needle into the colored rinsing water and drew the liquid into the syringe. He took the syringe out without expelling the water, put his hand up, squirted the water into his mouth, and swallowed.

Mike and Mark looked at each other. One raised an eyebrow; the other shook his head.

After the massive raids of the Short North, the media was invited into Nigleburger's house for the public to witness one of the drug scenes. They photographed the disgusting kitchen and filthy living room with pink streaks on the walls and ceilings from the colored water being squirted. Federal Judge James L. Graham from the southern district of Ohio tried the case regarding Roger. He made Roger wear a breathing mask to protect other people from possible contagions.

Sanbino

Mark and Mike continued to visit the residences of the Cubans, buying half a gram at a time. They visited Sanbino one time as he was preparing a steak. The scent of garlic greeted them as they entered his home. Welcoming both, Sanbino asked if they were hungry. Both thanked him but said no. Mike told him they had dropped by for half of a gram of cocaine. Sanbino said okay, that he would finish his steak and then weigh the cocaine out for them. Both Mike and Mark nodded and told him to take his time.

Sanbino turned back to the counter by the stove. On the counter, he had a saucer that had cocaine on it. A teaspoon was set on the saucer. Pointing at Mike with the spatula he had in his hand, he asked, "Eddie, you want a coka? Do coka?"

He gestured to Mark as well.

Mike and Mark both shook their heads no. Mike added, "Not right now. My nose has been bleeding."

Sanbino turned his steak over, then picked the teaspoon up, dipped it into the cocaine, held it to his nose, and snorted. Mike thought, *this is like the movie Scarface, but it's here for real.*

When he turned back to them white power rimmed his nose. After he returned the spoon to the saucer, he picked the saucer up and handed it to Mike. "Okay, I'll take it to the bathroom," Mike told him.

In the bathroom, Mike scooped the cocaine into an evidence vial he carried in his pocket. From his jacket, he took another small bottle containing Inositol and placed some of its powdery substance just inside his left nostril.

Mike came out of the bathroom, beaming. He walked up to Mark and said in English, "Enjoy this dude because it doesn't happen."

Mark smiled back and shook his head, both knowing Sanbino would not understand what Mike had just said.

They continued to buy from as many Cuban Nationals that they could so they could disrupt or dismantle the complete entity in the Short North area.

***

Another time, Mike and Mark went to another house on McMillan. Sanbino was there with two other Cubans and a new guy, *Martin Sullivan*.

As Mark and Mike entered, Sullivan and Sanbino were joking and laughing. Mike looked at Mark and raised an eyebrow. "Old friends?"

Mark shrugged.

Sullivan was leaned up against the counters and cupboards in the small kitchen when they came in. He straightened. His hands formed fists and his body took an aggressive stance as they stood there talking to Sanbino. Sullivan was a rough-looking guy. He was in his late 20s, early 30s, standing about five feet eight inches. He looked solid and muscular; his eyes squinted and his face angry.

It was apparent to both Mark and Mike; Sullivan considered them new and a threat. "Who are you guys? I don't know who the fuck you are, and I've been here forever. I've never seen you before."

Even after months of establishing themselves, Sanbino and his friends were looking suspiciously at Mike and Mark. The Cubans were trusting Sullivan and his instincts over them.

Mike took a defensive tone. "Dude, we're from North Columbus. We've been partying at the Caravan for a few months. We know the bartenders and people there."

Sullivan nodded to Sanbino and asked, "¿Policía?"

As if he had never seen them before, Sanbino fixed his glaring eyes on Mike and Mark

Sullivan gestured to Mike. "Come here. We just want to make sure you're cool. I want to talk to you."

Mike and Mark, now on guard, followed him. Mike went first, being mindful he had a gun on him. They were told by superiors a while ago to carry small .32 automatics. They were like pea shooters. A person would have to be close to someone to do any damage, but at least it would provide some semblance of protection. In the Short North, everyone carried guns. Even if he were patted down, the .32 would not automatically alert Sullivan or Sanbino. It could buy Mike some time if he needed it.

Sullivan walked into a small, tight bedroom. Mike stopped just inside the door. Somehow, Sanbino was directly behind Mike nudging him inside. Another Cuban closed the folding door, leaving him and Mark outside the bedroom. Divided, they were losing control of the situation.

Training and experience taught them when it came to the time of purchasing; almost anything could happen. Mike was ready for the traffickers to pat him down. He searched his mind if he ever suggested he injected. They could demand to see track marks if he had. Answers to the question of "How do I know you're not the police?" ran through his mind. He waited for them to demand he drop to his underwear or see him take the drug. He was sandwiched between two people staring him down. Sullivan was the most threatening.

Only a few feet apart, with Sullivan on his left and Sanbino on his right, waiting to see Mike's reactions. Would he make a break for it? Is he sweating? Sullivan took out a piece of parchment folded into a gram envelope. He slowly opened the envelope and inside was a fine white powder. Mike cupped his right hand. He touched his middle finger to the cocaine, then brought his hand up to his mouth. He rubbed his gums with his index finger as he held the cocaine in place with his thumb.

At that moment, Sullivan's attitude changed. He believed Mike had tasted the coke. He handed the envelope to Sanbino and nodded. Sanbino opened the bedroom door and nodded to the Cuban with Mark.

Mark had been standing with his hands on his hips, intently listening. Seeing Mike come out smiling, he shifted into a more relaxed position. As he came out of the bedroom, Mike offered to buy the gram Sanbino was now holding.

All the occurrence was documented later that night, according to departmental policy. Mike let his supervisors know he had to simulate that he took cocaine.

***

Mark and Mike continued to hang out at The Caravan. Often, they would hear the name *Roberto Velazquez*. Their impression was that he was the key player in the conspiracy.

One night Mark and Mike were playing pool when a prostitute mentioned to one of the Cubans they were playing, Velazquez was in town. He had some good stuff that he was looking to move. Mike said, "Wow, we would love to get some of that if it hasn't been stepped on or worked on or adulterated with something."

Both Mark and Mike knew Velazquez didn't want to meet anybody. He wasn't the type to go out to bars and have sex with various prostitutes struggling with addiction. His activities and location were secretive. Listening to conversations at the bar, Mike had narrowed Velazquez's locale to a specific apartment complex, but he wasn't sure of the exact apartment. Plus, Velazquez was constantly moving around to avoid detection. He would send a girl to rent an apartment or house and only stay a month.

The prostitute looked at Mike, sizing him up, and then she eyed the others with him. "Let me make a phone call."

She walked away. She came back and asked, "He has a package. How much do you guys want?"

"I think we're willing to get a half an ounce for six hundred to seven hundred dollars," looking at Mark. Mark nodded.

She said to Mike, "Okay, let's go."

Mike went with her and another prostitute. Mark said he would stay at the Caravan.

They all climbed into Mike's car, and the girl directed him to a multi-unit complex with a large parking lot. She told him where she wanted him to park. Mike handed her a wad of money. As she got out of the passenger side, Mike glanced at a large black van on his left a few yards away. He watched the girl go down the sidewalk to the second building, open the front door, and enter. The van struck him as familiar. Looking closer, he recognized it as a Columbus Police SWAT van.

Mike thought, my *God, they're implementing a search warrant here.* He hoped the search warrant was for another building.

The girl was gone for about five to ten minutes when Mike saw two people exit the same building the girl had entered. As they went by one of the security lights, he read the words CPD Narcotics Unit glowing on their jackets.

Noticing Mike's car, the officers approached. He realized he knew them, specifically the female officer, since he had worked with her on another investigation. Mike rolled down his window. They shined their flashlights on him and the person in the backseat. The male officer said, "Why are you here?"

"I'm waiting for a buddy who's supposed to meet me here in the parking lot. We're going to a bar."

"Let's see your ID."

Mike gave him his undercover ID. "Who's in your backseat?"

"Just a friend of mine. She's my buddy's girlfriend."

"Let's see her ID."

The girl handed Mike her ID, and Mike gave it to the cop. "Stay here."

They walked over to the van. The female officer said something to her partner. He turned to look at Mike again and nodded. Mike knew she had recognized him. The male opened the door of the van and got on the radio. Mike knew he was checking the girl's ID for warrants. He could hear the dispatcher's voice as she gave him the information.

They returned to Mike's vehicle and handed Mike the IDs. The male officer said, "You need to leave this general area. A search warrant is being executed."

Mike started the car and glanced to see if the other girl was on her way. No one was coming, so he left.

Later, the girl who had Mike's money walked into The Caravan and came straight to him. She was still shaking from her experience. "I walked down the hallway and, suddenly, here come guys wearing SWAT uniforms. They wanted to know what I was doing there. I thought they were going to take your money. They took my ID and then called it in. Thank God there weren't any warrants on me. They didn't take your money. I told them I was there to visit my aunt in the building.

Thank God I wasn't in Roberto's apartment five minutes before, because that SWAT team would have been on top of me."

She handed Mike's money back to him as she told her story.

After roll call the next day, Mike called the Narcotics Unit of the Columbus Police Department.

They apologized for stepping into an ongoing case. Usually, the Sheriff's Narcotic Unit, the Columbus Narcotic Unit, and the State police would coordinate their efforts to avoid conflict. But the present sheriff would not allow the deputies to communicate with the CPD unit. He didn't trust it. Since Mike was working undercover under the jurisdiction of the Department of Drug Enforcement Administration, he felt it was okay to check and see what had occurred the night before. The DEA provided the money for his partner and him to buy drugs from the Cubans.

The Columbus police arrested Roberto Vasquez that night with a small amount of cocaine, but they didn't get nearly enough to indict him for his other major infractions. Luckily, Vasquez was convicted of drug trafficking, but he did not receive time for his part in distributing drugs that he would have if Mike and Mark had gathered more evidence.

The Investigation continued for five months. Eventually, they would indict twenty people. Twelve were Cuban Nationals. The Cubans were buying large quantities of cocaine from other Cubans out of Miami and Detroit, Michigan. They were transporting back and forth, sometimes using the prostitutes from the Short North; other times, they used locals from Florida and Michigan to not raise suspicion.

When they executed the raids in this area, the team could not locate Sanbino Ruiz. It wasn't until months later, when Mike was driving through the Short North in another undercover vehicle, that he saw Sanbino walking down the sidewalk. He radioed a police cruiser that was nearby. Lieutenant Paul Tobinski, a friend of Mike's, was driving the cruiser. He met him on the street.

"The guy walking right down the street there is Sanbino Ruiz. I have federal warrants for his arrest."

Tobinski helped Mike arrest Sanbino right on High Street, the main street in the Short North. They grabbed him and placed cuffs on him. As Mike put him in the police car, Sanbino looked up and said, "You did a good job. I did not know you were policía."

Most Cubans they arrested in the Short North raid worked out a plea agreement in the Columbus U.S. Federal Court. Some instigated the Prison Riots and Hostage Crisis outside Atlanta in 1987, where twenty-three were injured, and one inmate was killed. The overcrowding conditions of the prison, holding "47% more than its supposed capacity," and their anger over the government's deal to deport many of them back to Cuba, are said to have caused the uprising. It lasted eleven days and involved 120 hostages. Three buildings of the facility were lost to fire.

Part Four

Shawn

Shawn

Shawn was raised in the small town of Grove City, about ten miles from Columbus, Ohio. Married immediately out of high school, public service became a goal for him. His strong and religious mom gave him the idea to apply for deputy sheriff. He applied and was hired initially as a dispatcher and became a communication officer in 1985.

In January 1986, he realized his goal after he went to the Franklin County Sheriff's Training Academy. Before his twenty-first birthday, his status changed from communication officer to deputy sheriff. The learning curve was steep. Two years later, a patrol opening occurred, and he was selected for the patrol division. At twenty-two years old, he was ten years younger than any other officer on his shift. At one point, everyone had to show their driver's license, and Shawn's license still displayed "co-signed by mother." It took a while for Shawn to live that down.

Part of the many transitions Shawn had to make was to use his brain instead of his brawn. In high school, Shawn was known to never back down from a fight. In school and around the surrounding area, he was respected to hold his own. As a patrol officer, he had to learn a new set of rules of respect. He couldn't take a swing at someone because they called him a name. He learned from the veterans how to talk to people.

Shawn first came to know Mike Powell when Mike taught his academy classes concerning the identification of illegal substances and their handling. When he was on patrol, he would be assigned to security when narcotics search warrants were executed. He would also transport perpetrators that were arrested to jail or to the detective bureau to be interviewed.

His next encounter with Mike was when he stopped an individual with a suspended license. Because of the suspended license, he had probable cause to search the individual's car. Shawn discovered a kilo of cocaine in the trunk. The department called in the narcotic's special investigation unit and that included Mike Powell.

About a year after he was involved in that arrest, the narcotic's special investigations unit posted four openings. Shawn applied. Mike was a supervisor assigned to interview, which included a home visitation. Because of the nature of the job as an undercover officer, the family had to be included in the interview. Shawn was selected for one position.

Shawn threw himself into his new role. In his mind, he became an actor who had the freedom to drive an undercover car, be out of uniform, grow his hair, a beard, and wear earrings. He took on roles of a drug addict, a burglar, drug trafficker, thief, and even a murderer. His competitive side was revealed when he decided it would be his goal to produce results in more cases than anyone else in the unit. He put in long hours, did paperwork at home, and did everything he could to be successful.

Being dedicated to work and being an undercover officer had its downside. Shawn would occasionally embarrass his wife and kids. He once went to a parent/teacher conference with long stringy hair, a beard, wearing an earring, and grubby clothes. After the meeting, he realized the teacher must have thought he was a real dirt ball dad.

He did his best to rearrange his work schedule to make school and sporting events, but many times, they were missed. Often, he would be out to dinner with his family, and his beeper would go off, and he'd have to leave. Weekend plans were scrapped at the last minute because of a drug raid. Holidays were done without him because of a drug buy that couldn't wait. In 2007, his marriage ended, another casualty of undercover work.

Diamond Jim

Normally in Pickaway County, the Sheriff has total police jurisdiction of municipalities, villages, and townships, but in this situation, he had called on Franklin County's sheriff for help. With a population of around 56,000 over 507 square miles, he didn't have the manpower to take on the following operation. Although the county boasts of the world-famous Circleville Pumpkin Festival and many recreational opportunities, they weren't quite ready to handle the recreational activities of one *Diamond Jim*.

Under Mike Powell's supervision, Shawn was teamed up with a new agent, *Patrick*. An informant had paved the way for them to buy cocaine in rural areas of Pickaway County. Since this was Shawn's hometown area, he had high expectations to take down the operation.

Diamond Jim had a law enforcement history of his own, but not one expected of a drug dealer. Diamond Jim was a former sergeant for the Ohio Highway Patrol. For his retirement, Jim had become head of a cocaine fencing organization.

Shawn and Patrick had an informant telling them about a house in the country where Diamond Jim was selling to "approved" clients who showed up at his door with cash or stolen items. The first step to these types of operations was to cut the informant out and establish an undercover as a backup. Patrick had already established himself using the informant. Now he was to set up Shawn, now identified as Tony, as backup and the money man.

The house in the country was less a risk than a house in the city. It was in a small rural community that only had dilapidated houses and trailers. The tiny, unassuming house was perfect for Diamond Jim's purposes because it was off a major rural highway accessible to customers. Since it was the last house in this community, Patrick and Shawn had to drive down a long dirt lane to see the top of the house on their approach. No one was around to count or notice a flow of traffic.

As they drove from Columbus, Patrick kept rehearsing his lines. "This is what I'm going to say…." Over and over.

The directions were simple. Patrick was to approach the door of the house and answer the question, "Who is it?"

Pulling up to the house, no other car was in the driveway. Shawn was driving. He put the car in park and surveyed the house. It could have been hand built by the original owner. It was a two-story white siding house that days of pristine and loving care were over. Patrick, distracted, was still practicing his lines in his head.

Shawn clapped Patrick on the shoulder and said, "Okay, let's do this."

Both exited the car at the same time. Shawn, fixed on the house, let Patrick go up the concrete stoop first to knock on the wooden black streaked door. No movement could be seen, but both knew they were eyed through the small diamond-shaped window high on the door. "Who is it?"

"Patrick and Shawn."

Shawn registered the mistake of his real name for the undercover name of "Tony" as he took a swipe at his beard with his hand, leaning his head to the side but not losing sight of the door out of the corner of his eye.

The metal scrape and click of the deadbolt was distinct.

Coming from the light of the outside to the darkness of the living room was unnerving. Shawn hid the feeling by taking off his sunglasses. He glanced at Patrick to see if he was masking his nerves. Patrick had kept his glasses on and stood with hands at his side.

Standing in front of them was the man who Patrick had described. Here was Diamond Jim. Still in good shape, gray streaking through his hair, Jim stood with his hands on the sides of his belt. It's the stance a lot of former police relax to from years of having so much equipment on their belts. Next to him, the man who had answered the door, Diamond Jim's "doorman" *Steve*. Diamond Jim invited them to the small dining area connected to the front room to the left. Shawn noted in the flicker of an old tube TV, the old couch and two armchairs with snatches of white at the arms. The musty smell of the room had to be coming from the rug, worn in the areas they were invited to walk. Over his shoulder he noted stairs that led to the upstairs.

Diamond Jim invited them to sit at a worn dining room table. Patrick sat across from Diamond Jim, now at the head of the table. Shawn sat awkwardly on Diamond Jim's left on one of the two mismatched side chairs. The chair's seat had lost its padding, and he sank into the hollow remains of the seat. Jim was leaning forward checking both Patrick and Shawn out. "What can I do for you boys?"

"I need an 'oz' to start. You come recommended by Patrick here," said Shawn. Shawn nodded to Patrick.

Shawn glanced at the certificate that hung on the wall behind Diamond Jim. The logo of the wings and tire was distinct. Retired was in bold print. Diamond Jim caught his distraction. He turned to look where he knew Shawn was looking. He jutted his thumb at the certificate. "Yup. Twenty-five years. Retired Sergeant Ohio State Highway Patrol."

Shawn said, "Damn man, I ain't here to get busted or something, you still the cops, man?"

Jim smiled and seemed relaxed back into his chair. "Nah, man. I ain't with them anymore. You ain't got anything to worry about."

Shawn felt like they had forgone the "Are you a cop?" conversation by reversing things on Diamond Jim.

Yelling to Steve, Jim instructed him to take Shawn and Patrick to order the product.

As the guys left the house, Steve seemed to automatically lead the way to his car. "You drive," he said to Patrick.

"No, my car, I drive," said Shawn.

Steve shrugged and waited for Shawn to hit the button to let him in the back. Patrick and Shawn exchanged looks over the car hood.

They drove about three miles to a full-service gas station. Steve told Shawn to pull near a pull up phone booth. He told

Shawn to park about five feet away, got out of the back seat and, after looking around, punched some numbers on the pay phone.

"Hey, I need two boxes of Cheerios. Yeah, two. Okay."

Steve had ordered two ounces of cocaine. One for Patrick and Shawn and one for Diamond Jim. Jim had a lot of customers who were not as patient as Patrick and Shawn, so he had to have product on hand.

Backing officers up in this rural area was hard. The seclusion of the area plus the lack of places to hide was a tough challenge. As Patrick and Shawn went back to the house to wait for the drop, both were mindful of the difficulties of keeping them safe. At least with having to use the phone at the gas station, the narcotic surveillance team could check on them.

Making conversation on the way back to the house, Shawn mentioned how busy the gas station was. Steve said, "Yeah, they have a safe full of money. As soon as me and Jim can find a crew, we're gonna break in over some night and take the safe."

Shawn said, "Damn, that sound like "good work" there."

"Hey, if you guys are interested, let Jim know," Steve said.

On their return to the house, Patrick and Shawn moved from the dining room to the brightly lit kitchen and stayed there for forty-five minutes, waiting for the supplier to arrive. They hoped that their surveillance team would have a chance to copy the tag number of the supplier's car and send it back to Columbus. When the supplier arrived, Patrick nor Shawn had a chance to see the supplier. He delivered the product, backlit by the sun at the front door.

Diamond Jim was happy with this smooth deal. Shawn was considered a big spender in this circle. Most of the customers in this rural area could only buy smaller amounts. His usual customers were trading stolen property, which means Jim would have to fence it out to get his money. The usual amount for this operative was small. The big spenders, like Shawn, were helping his business and his profit margin grow.

The next buy from Diamond Jim happened in the dark of a winter's evening. This time, as they drove up to the little house, they could see dozens of cars. Once Shawn and Patrick had been identified, they walked into a crowded, solidly packed living room. Everyone inside was partying. Beer was flowing. The air was dense from folks smoking weed. Pills were being swallowed. Everyone there was waiting for the cocaine from the supplier.

"Hey, you guys want two ounces? Man. The supplier's coming down, but I'm not sure how much he's bringin'. Steve take these guys to the pay phone. See where he's at. See if he can bring down a few more ounces."

Same drill. Shawn drove. Patrick was shotgun. Steve rode in the back. It turns out the supplier hadn't left his house yet.

"Hey, can you bring a couple more boxes of Cheerios down? Yeah, sure."

Driving back, Shawn was trying to develop what to say or do since the house was full of partying people. They were going to have an eerie situation. Undercovers are put in a disreputable position in cases like this.

What if a joint is passed around? If he or Patrick don't smoke, they'll look like cops. They both knew they were going to be on the spot because they knew how long the supplier takes to come from Columbus.

Back at the house, the lone light in the living room remained to be the television. The haze of smoke had increased with an increase in people. But now, people were going outside; the stuffiness of the house was getting to them. Patrick and Shawn stayed standing in the living room's darkness, making conversation with some of the other folks. Steve came up and offered them both a beer. Gladly, they both accepted. Twenty-five minutes dragged along. Gradually, they had managed to get close to the front door. Shawn was hoping to glimpse the supplier as he came in, even if it was only by the dim lighting.

He hardly noticed the knock on the door. Steve came through the few people to ask his question. "Who is it?"

Shawn clearly heard, "Rhonda and Jim." Recognizing the voice, he stood behind the opening door. Rhonda and Jim were his aunt and uncle. Shawn was from this area growing up, but he never imagined he would see his aunt or uncle or any other of his relatives during this operation. Patrick noticed his movement but thought nothing of it.

As the door closed, Shawn turned to move deeper into the living room. Patrick stayed where he was hoping to glimpse the dealer. As Rhonda and Jim entered the house, Shawn pretended to listen to another person's conversation as they passed him. Luckily, they never even glanced at him. Shawn made his way to the couch up against the wall where the television light was the dimmest. He watched his aunt say something to his uncle. She went into the brightly lit kitchen. Uncle Jim turned and walked straight to where Shawn was sitting. Shawn prayed that the five or six years they hadn't seen each other had faded his memory of what he looked like. Shawn had dressed his part. His hair was long, and he was sporting a beard and earrings. His aunt knew he was a cop. He also knew she might have been drinking and would not think to keep quiet.

His uncle made his way to the only other seat in the living room. Right next to Shawn.

"Howdy."

Shawn took a swig of what remained of his now warm beer and nodded. His uncle started talking about the television show that was on and how much better it looked on his television. Shawn kept his end of the conversation up for fifteen-twenty minutes. Luckily, his uncle was already trashed.

Finally, Patrick signaled the supplier was there.

Diamond Jim took the cocaine from the supplier and disappeared to break it down where no one could see him.

When Diamond Jim returned to the kitchen, Aunt Rhonda called Uncle Jim into the kitchen.

"Jim, come into the kitchen and give me the money!"

Uncle Jim groaned. Steading himself as he rose from the low under stuffed couch, he said, "That woman is so bossy."

Shawn just nodded.

It was a long five more minutes before Aunt Rhonda and Uncle Jim came out of the kitchen and made their way out of the house.

As Shawn's aunt and uncle went out the front door, Diamond Jim yelled to Shawn and Patrick to get their buy. Shawn winced. He hoped his relatives didn't connect his name. Shawn could feel the sweat going down the middle of his back as he counted out the $2300 for their two ounces.

As they drove down the long, steep driveway, Patrick noticed Shawn was shaky and looking pale. "What the hell had been going on, man?"

"You know that last couple that came into the house?"

"No, I was watching for the supplier."

"That was my drunk aunt and uncle. My uncle was sitting next to me on the couch."

"You're shitting me. And he didn't recognize you? Or did he know it was you and said nothing?"

"I think he was so drunk he didn't realize it was me. But my aunt, if she had connected my name as they headed out the door, we would have been toast."

Both were laughing as they pulled onto the highway, going back to Columbus.

During the debriefing, Shawn and Patrick didn't tell their supervisor, Sergeant Mike Powell, about the relative encounter. He would have immediately replaced them.

Mike, Patrick, and Shawn planned a few more dope deals. Their goal was to take down the operation, arrest Diamond Jim, and anyone else in the house. The Pickaway County Sheriff arranged for a search warrant.

The game plan was set. The SWAT team was running surveillance. Patrick and Shawn needed to buy the cocaine one more time. Everybody was ready.

Patrick and Shawn went down that long driveway once more. They knocked on the door. Steve answered with his question. "Who is it?"

They went in and were greeted by Diamond Jim. Shawn noticed there were a few people in attendance, but not nearly as many as the night that he saw his aunt and uncle. He made a quick pass to make sure his aunt and uncle were not there. Once again, Diamond Jim sent Steve to make the three-mile drive to order their two ounces. Diamond Jim needed the supply he had for his Friday customers. The country dive bars were going to be hopping. People would come to Diamond Jim's first.

Shawn and Patrick got in their car, drove the three miles to the gas station, and heard Steve order three to four boxes of Cheerios.

By the time they returned, the other folks had cleared out. It was only Shawn, Patrick, Steve, and Diamond Jim sitting around the kitchen table. Jim was throwing around a knife. Finally, he took out some remaining cocaine, stuck the knife in the bag, and placed the cocaine on the tip of the knife. He was about to snort it when he suddenly looked at Shawn and said, "Hey, you want some of this? It's like Peruvian gold."

Shawn said, "Nah man. I'm good. I have to drive all the way back to Columbus. With two ounces of cocaine on me, dude, I sure don't want to be stopped."

"That's cool." Diamond Jim said.

Patrick asked him about the Highway Patrol retirement certificate. "Yeah, I used to be a cop. But you know? That life is for suckers. I'm so much better off now than when I was with the highway patrol up in Columbus. I'm doubling my intake. You know, having all that experience with the highway patrol, you know…"

He stopped and pointed the knife at Patrick. "I can spot a cop a mile away. That's why they'll never catch me."

Just then, his phone started to ring. People were calling. People were coming in and out of the house. Diamond Jim was telling them his guy was on his way.

After a long hour's wait, Diamond Jim went out to meet his supplier. But he didn't return. Patrick and Shawn sat tight.

Suddenly, a customer ran into the house panicking, "Steve, the cops got Diamond Jim and another dude. Cops are everywhere! They're coming! They're coming!"

Steve said to Patrick and Shawn, "Guys, you need to get out of here."

Patrick said, "No doubt."

With that, Patrick and Shawn went out the back door, carefully made their way to their car, and drove away.

At the briefing later, Patrick and Shawn found out that the supplier had spotted a police car on the way down to Diamond Jim's house. When Diamond Jim came outside, the supplier drove up and told him what he saw. Diamond Jim hopped in the car, and they drove to a cemetery close by to do business. That's where Mike and the squad met and arrested them.

In one hour, Pickaway County Sheriff's department served the warrant on Diamond Jim's house and recovered stolen property Jim had taken in on trade. Days later they served a warrant at the supplier's house in Columbus and found several ounces of cocaine and more stolen property.

Several months later, Patrick and Shawn testified at the trial of Diamond Jim. Diamond Jim was sentenced to ten years in prison.

Casanova

Shawn and his partner, Patrick, received an assignment concerning a complaint that a stripper was selling drugs out of a business on the west side of Columbus. The strip club was just a hole in the wall, a block building long and rectangular in an area that was continually having to deal with robberies, theft, and drug trafficking.

Patrick and Shawn paid the cover fee as they strolled in. It was a dimly lit place. No alcohol, only water, and sodas, which meant in Columbus, the strippers could go bare. They surveyed the place. It was typical for this type of establishment. The stage was in the middle of the room, and seating was around the stage. The bar stretched to the side and tables filled the rest of the space. Patrick and Shawn walked up to the stage seating and settled in a place. They watched a few dancers do their performances. During the first song, the dancers were fully clothed; the second they danced their clothes off to bathing suit/ bikini level, then during the third or fourth song, they would end up naked. The patrons would throw dollar bills on stage or put the dollars in the stripper's G-string as she danced.

The goals of the strippers were to get as much money off the patrons as they could. Once they were off the dance stage, they would mingle. The patrons would buy them a five to ten-dollar conversation drink of water or soda. This allowed the patron to talk to the stripper for five or ten minutes. The next goal of the stripper would be to persuade the patron to buy a private dance. The private dances ranged from twenty to fifty dollars. Tiny rooms in the back were set up for the private dances. This strip club was of the lower-level variety, so the women could make maybe a couple of hundred dollars a night.

One stripper seemed to gravitate toward Shawn during her dance performance. Star was probably in her early 20s. She had silky brown hair. She was heavy for a stripper. Shawn noticed stretch marks, so he knew right there she had children. He obliged her during her dance with dollar bills. After her dance, she mingled with patrons who declined when she asked them for a conversation drink. She made her way to Shawn, who answered, "Sure."

Patrick and Shawn had set their goal for the evening to make conversation with as many dancers as they could, so Patrick was also buying conversation drinks for dancers. They were a good team. Shawn was athletically built, dark-haired and dark eyed. Patrick was lean and tall, blond, and blue eyed. They hoped to steer the discussions toward whether drugs were being sold. Both guys were dressed as construction workers in flannel shirts, dirty jeans, work boots, and worn baseball caps.

"What's your name, and what do you do?"

"Tony. I work construction."

"Always been in Columbus?"

"I was raised south of here. How about you?"

"Yeah, me too. Do you party?"

"A little. I smoke a little weed; do a bit of coke. How about you?"

"My roommate does cocaine, but I don't. I like to smoke weed now and then."

Shawn had to buy a few conversation drinks for Star since if he didn't, she would be inclined to get up and move. If she didn't, the manager would come over and tell her to move on. After a few of those drinks, Star left Shawn to do her second performance.

They stayed for a few hours. Because of their conversation about partying, Shawn wanted to stay in touch with Star. He asked when she would perform again before he left.

"I'll be back in a few days," she said, smiling up at him.

"Good. I'll be back to see ya."

Shawn and Patrick returned a few nights later. Patrick had also picked up a lead or two, so they thought they had a good start. They followed the same plan. Shawn bought some conversation drinks for other dancers. He found they didn't want to talk about anything to do with drugs. If they did, they were users, not traffickers. Patrick was finding the same thing.

"Hey, guy. You're cheating on me?"

Shawn turned to see Star smiling down at him. Smiling broadly at her, he put his hands up and said, "Well, no. But sit. Let me buy you a drink."

Star sat. "How've you been?"

"Fine. Keepin' busy. Greg (Patrick) and I were looking for weed, but we couldn't find any, so we thought we'd stop by to relax."

"Well, I can hook you up with some weed."

"Really?"

"Sure! I don't have any on me today, but I can get some for you. It's pretty good weed. I can get it from my roommate. I'm working tomorrow night again. Stop in?"

"Star, you're an angel. Sure."

"How much you want?"

"Can you get me a half an ounce?"

"Sure, I can, Tony. I can do that. I'll have it here waiting for you."

"Cool. Thanks, Star."

They didn't stay too much longer after that. Patrick and Shawn were happy to get a step forward in the investigation. Patrick had struck out.

They returned the following night after spending the day working on other cases, reviewing reports, and listening to recorded conversations. After watching Star's performance, she came down and sat with them. Shawn bought her a drink. After a brief chit chat, she asked, "Do you still want the weed?"

"Yeah."

"Here's the key to my car. It's the gray Camaro in the parking lot. It's in the console between the seats. Just leave the money in there."

Shawn took her keys and went to the parking lot. The Camaro was an older model, slightly beat up. Shawn opened it, and in the light inside, he saw a baby and toddler seat speckled with crumbs. Smiling to himself, he knew those seats himself. After opening the console, he found the bag of marijuana and replaced it with the amount of money they had agreed on. He exited the car, made sure he locked it. He went back into the club and returned her key to her and to find Patrick.

"Everything go okay?" Star asked.

"Yeah, sure. Everything's fine. I got it."

"Inside that bag is my phone number, Tony. Call me? After I get off work at midnight, we could have some drinks."

Shawn smiled at her. "Nah, it's already ten. I got to go home. Work tomorrow."

Back in the car, Patrick teased him. "I think she's into you, man."

Shaking his head, Shawn said, "She must have thought by going out to the car, if I was a cop, I couldn't arrest her for anything."

Patrick shrugged. "A lot of people think that."

Shawn called her after a day and asked her when she would work again. After a bit of idle chat, he asked her if she could get more weed. She said sure.

The next time, the pattern was the same. He went out to her car, took out the weed, and replaced it with money. This time, in their conversation, Star mentioned her kids. Shawn said he had some but was divorced. He tried to stay away from personal things, but she was determined to find out more about him.

Patrick and Shawn decided later that night as they wrote their reports, it was time for Shawn to see if he could get another drug from her. It would increase the severity of the indictment. The goal was not to arrest her, but to make this all worthwhile, he had to see if he could get a line on a more serious trafficker and her supplier. For Star, this was a way to supplement her income and pay some bills. He suspected she was supplying others at the club.

When he talked to her again, he leaned forward close to her and said, "When we first met, you mentioned your roommate liked some white (cocaine). Do you think you can get some?"

She responded by leaning closer to him, "Yeah, I can get you some white."

"Can you get me an eight ball?"

"I don't know. I can check."

Star stood and went back to the dressing room. When she came back ten minutes later, Shawn had a fresh drink waiting for her. She leaned into him again. "I can't get you a ball. But I can get you a gram or a teen."

"Yeah, I'll take a teenager."

Shawn hung out, talking to other dancers for about an hour. Star tapped the shoulder of the dancer Shawn and Patrick were laughing with. She stood and walked away, and Star sat. "Let me order you a drink."

"No, don't. I gotta go get ready for my next set. It's outside waiting for you. My roommate just dropped it off."

"Sweet!"

Shawn took her key, went out to her car, and found the powder cocaine just as they had agreed. He placed $110 in her console.

Now they had three counts on her. Patrick and Shawn decided to get one more buy of cocaine from her. It was time to wrap up this small buy investigation or take it to the next level. He made one more call to find out if she could get another teen for him. She said she could.

Later that week, per their arrangement, Shawn returned to the strip bar alone. He watched Star dance. As she flirted and winked at him, he threw dollar bills along with other patrons. After her performance, she came to where he was sitting.

"Where's your key?"

Star hesitated. "Do you want to have a private dance?"

Shawn sat back. This was the first time she had changed their plan. "Don't you have it?"

She smiled but seemed nervous. "Yes, I do but I've got a surprise for you."

"Alright. Let's do a private dance for twenty bucks."

She grabbed his hand and led him back to a private room. She asked him to sit on a chair and stepped on the small platform that served as a stage. As the music started, she stripped down. She bumped, ground, twerked, and played with her hair to the music. As she danced, Shawn could see a small bag of cocaine working its way out of her vagina. Star was laughing and playing with her breasts. Shawn, disgusted, was trying to go along laughing with her. He was thinking, *how do I pick up the bag of cocaine with her DNA all over it?*

Shawn had brought in a cup of coffee and a napkin. As Star turned her back to him to redress, Shawn leaned over and grabbed the bag of cocaine with the napkin, wrapped it, and put it in his pocket. When she was ready, she looked for the packet on the floor. "I've got it in my pocket," Shawn said.

As they left the private room to go back to the main area, Star turned to Shawn and asked, "What do you think?"

"That was pretty cool."

Star confronted him. "Tony, when are we going out for drinks?"

Shawn paused. "Yeah, okay. Let's go out and get some drinks. I'll call you."

Back at the office, Shawn told Patrick what happened.

"Jesus!"

"I know. It was something. How are we going to wrap this up? It's got to happen soon."

After making out their reports for the night, which included impounding the packet of cocaine wrapped in a napkin, Shawn came up with a plan.

Shawn would ask Star out for a date, but without her knowing it, Patrick would also be there. Shawn couldn't afford for her to think he was really interested in her. He would meet her at a restaurant with a bar, and after a drink, he would ask her if she wanted to smoke some weed before dinner. All three would then go out to the parking lot, and an arrest team would be out there and arrest all three of them to avoid Star freaking out in the parking lot.

Patrick thought it was a good plan, but asked, "Kind of cheesy way to get out of paying for a meal, isn't it, Shawn?"

Shawn shrugged and laughed.

Patrick and Shawn walked into the restaurant, and a hostess led them to a booth. Star came in after about ten minutes.

Star, dressed for their date, looked classy, with a lovely dress and heels. Shawn felt rotten. He realized this date meant a lot to her. She scooted into the booth close to Shawn. "Greg, I didn't know you would be here."

Drinking some water, Patrick said, "I met Tony here thinking I would get takeout, but I decided against it. I was getting ready to leave."

Shawn put his hand up and said, "Stay for a bit and have a drink with us."

Star's eyes registered confusion. She placed her hand on Shawn's bicep and said, "Are you afraid of me, Tony? "

They all laughed. Patrick shaking his head, said, "This was great, but I've gotta go."

"Okay, but why don't we all go out and have a smoke before you leave?" Shawn suggested.

Star raised her eyebrows. "You got some?"

Shawn nodded. Star smiled. "I do too!"

"Well, we can smoke yours or smoke mine. It don't matter." Shawn answered.

They all slid out of the booth and headed to the parking lot. Under the view of the arrest crew, Patrick sat in the back of Shawn's car. Shawn opened the door for Star on the passenger side. Star opened her purse. "Tony, do you want to smoke yours or mine?"

"We can smoke mine."

She was startled when detectives rapped on the windows on both sides. "Who's that?" She snapped.

"I don't know."

A badge appeared up against Shawn's window. "Oh, my God! It's the cops!"

Star's eyes were wide. She rolled down the window. Two hands and a head appeared in her window. "We need you all to step out of the vehicle."

Looking confused, they all got out of the car.

Shawn said, "What can we do for you officers?"

A female officer patted down Star and checked her purse, taking out her marijuana. She showed the other officers. Two other cops patted down Shawn and Patrick and asked for their IDs. The female officer took Star aside and told her there was a warrant out for her arrest for trafficking in marijuana and cocaine. Star, in a shrill voice, said, "I borrowed that purse from my roommate. I don't know what you're talking about."

The officers cuffed them all and took them down to the Sheriff's Detective office. *Detective Sargent Marley Warren* took

Star into the interrogation room to question her. She tried to find out who her dealer was and offered if she cooperated, it could lessen her charges. Shawn and Patrick sat outside the interview room at their desks.

After about an hour, Marley came out of the interrogation room, shaking her head. "You won't believe how much she's protecting you two. I asked her if you were who she was getting her supply from. She said no. She said you're friends and insisted you're not drug dealers or even drug users! She's protecting you guys to the hilt! I think you are going to have to tell her you're undercover. She denies selling. What do you think?"

They sat there for a bit. Patrick, looking at Shawn, shook his head and shrugged. Shawn said, "Yeah, Marley, go ahead. Let her know we're undercover."

Marley went back into the interrogation room, sat across from Star, and quietly said, "Star, I have to tell you something. Those two guys who were in the car with you they're undercover detectives."

Star brought her chin up and said, "No way. Those two are not undercover cops. They both work construction for Kokosing. Tony told me so. I know a cop when I see one."

Marley opened the door. "She doesn't believe me. Why don't you two come in."

Shawn went in first, and Patrick followed. Star's mouth formed an O. "No f-ing way. You guys are really cops?"

Both Shawn and Patrick had their badges on their belts and IDs attached to their shirts. Star's eyes were level with Shawn's badge. Her eyes filled with tears. "But I loved you, Tony. I loved you. I thought you loved me."

Marley tried to calm her. She handed her a tissue and asked her if she could get her water or coffee. Shawn walked out and sat at this desk, shaking his head. Marley walked into the office, leaving the door open and asked Patrick to keep an eye on Star. She leaned on Shawn's desk and said, "Well, Casanova, remember you were only doing your job."

Shawn looked up at Marley and shook his head.

Suddenly, they heard Star, shrill and angry, say," I could punch him in the face. A date! A date! He said this was a date! No wonder you were there! I never thought you guys were cops! You guys should be on TV. You guys should be TV detectives!"

Star continued to refuse to give up her roommate or her roommate's connection. Star, charged with four counts of trafficking with two counts for marijuana and two counts for cocaine, ended up with probation and a fine.

Liz and the Ice Cream Man

When working in Narcotics, many of the cases come from public complaints. The undercover and his team decide how to approach each complaint. He can try to find an informant to collect information, set surveillance to determine what the situation is, or he can do a cold buy, which is approaching the subject of the complaint and trying to work his way in the door.

This complaint that Shawn was assigned concerned a woman in an apartment complex selling crack cocaine out of her third-floor apartment. The address led Shawn to a brick apartment building that had scissored stairs on the outside. During this hot, sticky August day, he could see adults and kids slowly going up and down the stairs. The doors of the apartments were on the face of the building, along with a single window. Presently, many people were sitting outside fanning themselves because the old building didn't have any or very little air conditioning. After sizing up the situation, Shawn went up to the suspect's apartment door to try a cold buy.

Shawn climbed the stairs and knocked on the door. A tiny, graying woman opened the door. She looked up at Shawn, squinting, "Who are you?"

Shawn smiled and pointed to himself. "Don't you remember me? I'm Tony."

"I don't remember you."

"Yeah, from the market a couple of days ago."

There was a small neighborhood market down the road where people could pick up staples. "You met me in the market a week ago. Don't you remember me?

"No."

"You gave me your address and told me to stop by sometime if I needed to be hooked up."

"I don't remember you. I meet a lot of people and talk to a lot of people, and I don't remember you."

"Well, I met you. It's alright. If you ain't got nothing or you don't wanna, um, if you don't wanna hook me up, I'll leave."

She stood back a bit and looked up at his face. Shawn was five feet ten to her possible five. "Well, what are you looking for?"

"A forty piece." (A forty-dollar piece of crack cocaine.)

She smiled and raised an eyebrow. "I think I can hook you up with that."

She gestured for him to come inside her apartment. It was sweltering and smelled of cooking. Shawn was sweating before he went in, but this place was stifling, lacking any cross ventilation. Her apartment opened into a living room and kitchen area. In his experience, older women usually had knick-knacks and furniture. But this lady only had a stained couch, a faded chair, a small kitchen dinette table, and two chairs. Strangely, a couple of child's toys were on the stained carpet.

She gestured to Shawn. "Have a seat. "

He sat down at the kitchen table. On the table were envelopes and an ashtray containing Chore Boys Scrubbers©. Looking around, Shawn saw full ashtrays on the arms of the sofa and chair containing ashes and butts of cigarettes. He looked closer around his feet and saw burned bits of Chore Boys on the floor. He knew then he was in a user's house. Chore Boys Scrubbers© were used as a screen for crack, and in a user's place, bits of copper from the Chore Boys were always on the carpet and floor. It was essential for him to know when he went into a place if it was a seller's or a user's. If it was a user's place, the danger increases. The user may want the undercover to smoke to prove he's not a cop. More importantly, they were also unpredictable.

The woman had disappeared down the short hall. Shawn moved his head to peek around the corner to see if she was coming back. When she wasn't, he moved the envelopes around with his finger to see the name.

Elizabeth McAfee. He looked up when she came up back with two rocks of cocaine in a baggy.

Shawn took out his wallet and gave her two twenty-dollar bills. "Hey, do you want to smoke with me?" She asked.

"No, I'm cool right now. I'm going down the road to meet my girl. But maybe next time."

She nodded and pressed her lips together to form a frown. "That's alright. Maybe next time."

When Shawn left the apartment, he felt confident the cold buy had gone well. He went back to the office, and before he started his reports, he looked up her name in the database. He knew he had the right name when her picture came up. The drugs had taken their toll. She was only in her early fifties. Her face had thinned, her skin now pallid and grayish. The photo was from a previous arrest.

Shawn had to make some decisions. Was she small time? If he went into her place with a search warrant, what could he gain? He could arrest her and try to flip her to find out about her supplier. What will his next step be? In discussing it with the team, he decided to see how much she had in her house.

A few days later, Shawn returned to ask for an eight ball. An eight ball is an eighth of an ounce. 3.5 grams. The last time, the forty-piece was one-eighth of a gram. He needed to see what she had in her apartment.

Shawn went up to her door again and knocked. She answered, and he asked for an eight ball. She paused for a second and said, " Oh Tony, I don't have an eight ball here."
"Ah, you don't have an eight ball?" Shawn shifted, trying to look like a petulant teen.

"Nah, I can get you another forty-piece, but I don't have an eight ball."

Now Shawn knew she was minimal with selling crack. She sold at a very low level.

"I'm on my way out, Tony. Do you want a forty-piece?"

"Yeah, I'll take it. Hey, can you get me an eight ball?"

"Yes, I can. But you're going to have to call ahead. That way, I'll have it for you. I don't like to keep that much around."

Shawn took the forty-piece, knowing he had set up for the next buy. A few days later, he called her and told her he'd like that eight ball.

"When you coming by?"

"I'd like to come by in an hour."

"Okay, I'll call my boy now."

Shawn played this buy out. If he bought the eight ball, he would have a higher felony charge on her. He hoped by doing this; he could get her to cooperate with him to find the supplier.

He went over in thirty minutes instead of waiting an hour, hoping he might see her supplier.

Shawn pulled carefully into the parking lot. There were kids everywhere. He looked up and saw Liz in the doorway as if she was watching or expecting to see someone. Shawn walked up the stairs, and Liz met him at her door.

"Honey, he ain't here yet, but I'm expecting him any minute. You came early."

"I know. I'm sorry I gotta be at work, so I came early."

"No big deal. He'll be here in a few minutes."

Shawn and Liz stood in the doorway and talked for a few minutes about the sweltering weather when Shawn noticed kids running for the apartment stairs. He watched for a second and then heard the tinny jingle of an ice cream truck.

When the ice cream truck parked in the parking lot, the kids swarmed around it.

"There he is. Let's go."

"Where? Is he coming up?" Shawn turned and looked down the stairs.

"No, Tony. Follow me."

Shawn followed Liz down the stairs, through the parking lot, and to the ice cream man's truck still blaring happy jingles.

The ice cream truck was a renovated van. Shawn followed Liz as she went to the rear double doors. She stretched to open the doors with Shawn's help. Inside were a couple of benches and a few freezers.

The ice cream man, dressed in all white, including a white cap, saw Liz and motioned for her to come up. She sat on the back and swung her legs up and stood again with Shawn's help. The ice cream man stared at Shawn like 'who are you?'

He said nothing as he kept getting his pushups, cones, and popsicles out of the freezers and taking money. After he served all the kids, he reached up and pulled down the sliding side door. He climbed into the driver's seat and pulled out of the lot. Shawn hoped he was going to his next stop.

As he was driving, the ice cream man said, "Hey, girl, what do you need?"

"My boy here needs an eight ball, and I need one myself."

"Two balls, right?"

"Yes."

They pulled into the next apartment complex, and before he opened the sliding door for the kids, he reached into a cooler. Shawn could see him rooting around. He pulled out a bag that contained about an ounce of crack cocaine. He put the bag on a closed cooler and took out a scale and positioned it. Taking out the crack, he broke it down and weighed it to eight balls of 3.5 grams. He reached out to exchange an eight ball for money with Liz and did the same with Shawn. Without a word, the ice cream man turned and opened the sliding door and sold the kids their pushups, cones, and popsicles. He took them out from the same cooler he had stored the crack.

Once he took care of these kids, our driver pulled the side door closed, returned to the driver's seat. Shawn could sense Liz becoming edgy. She kept moving around on the bench. Her left hand, closest to Shawn, kept twitching. She asked our driver if he minded if she lit up.

"No, go ahead. I'll be just a few more minutes, and then I'll take you guys back."

Liz opened her small shoulder purse and took out a small glass tube with a Chore Boy remnant in it, along with a lighter. She next drew out a large yellow latex balloon. She turned to Shawn, who was watching her, and asked," Are you going to light up?"

"No, I didn't bring my stem. I'll wait."

"Okay."

Liz took her little crack stem in her right hand; then, she took a tiny piece of crack cocaine out her baggy and pushed it into her pipe. Deftly, she took the lighter and the balloon in her left hand, put the crack pipe to her mouth, and clicked the lighter. She breathed in almost pure 100% crack cocaine that she had vaporized. She held it in her lungs as long as she could until her body told her she had to exhale.

When she exhaled, she put the balloon up to her mouth and blew the vapor into it. She closed her eyes and waited for a few minutes for her body to absorb the first hit. Meanwhile, she pinched the balloon shut, saving the exhaled vapor from her lungs. After a bit, she took the balloon back to her lips and breathed in the contents for her second hit. She didn't want any of the vapors to go to waste. Liz had smoked one rock by the time the ice cream driver had finished his next stop and swung around to drop them off at Liz's apartment complex.

After Shawn helped Liz get down from the van. "Hey," he shook the ice cream man's hand. "Could I have your number so I can go through you directly?'

The man paused for a second. "No, let's continue going through Liz."

Shawn returned to the office to meet with Mike Powell and his other officers in the unit. He was worried the ice cream man was selling crack to kids along with his frozen treats. When asked, he had to say he hadn't seen him sell cocaine to kids or anyone else except Liz. The cocaine was in a separate bag in the cooler, so unless it leaked it wasn't likely to contamination the ice cream. They agreed there was no immediate risk in arresting this seller to take him off the street. They planned the weight of the buy and see how the investigation played out. The next time Shawn would go to Liz, he would ask for a half ounce, fourteen grams, or four eight balls.

Liz begged off. "I can't do a half ounce, Tony. You're going to have to go straight to my boy. I can't do half ounces."

With Shawn listening, she called her boy. "Do you remember the guy I was with that one time? You know the guy I brought you on that scorching day? Yeah. He wants a half ounce."

She said okay and hung up. "Tony, he says he can't do it today. But I'm to give you his number, and you can deal directly with him."

Shawn was pleased. He had wanted to cut Liz out because she was the smaller fish. The ice cream man was the larger trafficker.

Shawn called the ice cream man and set up a deal for the half ounce. Shawn and his supervisors decided they were going to do a buy-bust.

Shawn was to meet him in a parking lot away from where he sells his ice cream. No one wanted to do a buy-bust with kids around. Having police surrounding them with guns drawn was not a good idea. This surprise arrest needed to be done differently. The ice cream man agreed to meet Shawn in the parking lot of a convenient store. The chance he would sell ice cream there was minimal.

Shawn drove up to the parking lot of the convenient store, and there was his guy in his ice-cream van. Shawn, wearing a wire, went to the back of the truck and knocked. The ice cream man yelled that it's unlocked. Shawn looked around and counted two undercover cars parked on the street. He opened the double doors and hopped in. The ice cream man nodded to Shawn and went to the same cooler and brought out a baggy and a scale. After weighing out the fourteen grams, he placed it in small baggy and gave it to Shawn. Shawn gave the audio signal he had bought the crack cocaine.

As he opened the back doors to leave, the other narcotic policemen jumped in. The ice cream man did not resist. They read him his rights, handcuffed him, took him out, and placed him in one car. Shawn came back in to help search the van. They found a couple of ounces of crack cocaine in the refrigerated coolers and a handgun under the driver's seat.

Keg Room

The Keg Room was an old established bar in the Hilltop area. Modern multi-storied office buildings surrounded this dowdy brown stucco single-story building. The Hilltop was an assortment of smaller communities that feature historic and newer homes. It boasts to be one of the largest neighborhoods in the Ohio's capital city. It has an extensive history that spans from the original inhabitants of Native Americans to Camp Chase, a staging and training ground for the Union army during the Civil War and a Confederate prison camp, to the former home of the Columbus State Hospital for the Insane. The Hilltop had evolved, as many urban neighborhoods have, to where poverty has been caused by jobs leaving the area.

A person driving through the area could assume The Keg Room was the local neighborhood bar. In August of 1998, the sheriff's office received multiple complaints cocaine was being sold either by bartenders or they were looking the other way. The Franklin County Sheriff Department sent undercover detectives Shawn Bain and *Jerry Malone* to investigate the situation.

The deputies did some research before they went to investigate. The clientele of the bar was diverse. All ages. All races. The income range of the bar's patrons was pretty much the same as the area, low to middle income.

Shawn and Jerry walked in about 4:30 on a Friday afternoon. At this time, Shawn was considered the seasoned undercover cop. Jerry was relatively new and still taking his cues from Shawn. Both were wearing baggy jeans, tee shirts, flannel shirts plus work boots. Shawn had trimmed his hair from a mullet to a shorter look but kept a bit of a beard. Jerry was thinner built but still athletic looking. To avoid looking like a cop, he had pierced his ear, but only wore a gold stud.

They decided their cover story would be they were construction workers who just finished their day, and it seemed like a Friday afternoon was a good time to check the place out. The little-attached patio was not yet bustling, but about fourteen people were scattered between the bar, eight tables, two pool tables, and the patio. They decided to sit at the bar. A friendly thirty-ish female bartender greeted them with, "What can I get ya?"

The two of them were chatting it up with her, sipping beer about 15 – 20 minutes when two guys entered. In their early 20s, one was tall and skinny. He had a spooky Nosferatu-kind of look about him. His arm sleeve tattoo had several skulls, bats, and Jerry swore he saw the face of the original Barnabas Collins from Dark Shadows soap opera days. A spider web tattoo peeked out of his black t-shirt and crawled up his neck to his left ear. The other guy had more of a muscular look. He had short-cropped, curly dark-blond hair. He had his sleeves rolled up but only one tattoo, an old Cincinnati Reds logo: the wishbone C with REDS printed in the middle. The Nosferatu-guy was quiet, but his buddy made up for him. They walked over to the open pool table. It was about 50-feet from Shawn and Jerry. As they played pool, the other one cussed loud. He laughed loud. He talked loud. While they played, they kept eyeing Jerry and Shawn.

Jerry tilted his head towards them and asked the bartender, "What's with them?"

She snorted. "They're regulars. Don't mind *Rog*. He always acts that way toward new people. Like the place is his."

Shawn told Jerry he was going to put some quarters down to play the winner, a regular practice in most bars with pool tables. It allowed the pool players to know the winner was challenged to a game.

Shawn and Jerry were watching a Reds baseball game when they heard," Hey, you're up!"

Shawn stood and walked over to the pool table. The Nosferatu guy stepped aside to watch. It turned out Rog had won. Pretending to watch the baseball game, Jerry stayed at the bar. After Shawn racked the balls, Rog broke. After a turn or two, Rog asked Shawn what he did. "Construction," nodding toward Jerry, "we just got off work and decided we'd come in for a coldie. How about you two?"

"I'm unemployed. Odd jobs, some. I learn fast. What kind of construction do you do? Maybe you can help me get a job."

"Carpentry, mostly. What happened to your last job?"

"I came to work late one day after a night of partying. My boss didn't like me. He was always lookin' to get up my ass. He said I was still high. I wasn't. That was it."

"High?"

"Yeah. I like, ya know." Rog gestured with his two fingers pinched together up to his lips. "Do you smoke?"

Shawn nodded. "Yeah, I do."

Shawn paused to look at the table to plan his next shot. He wanted to come with a chance to look serious, but not exactly shoot the lights out of the game.

"Have any on you?"

Shawn called his shot. "Three ball in the side pocket. Nah, I don't. I just got off work. The supervisors watch guys real close. It's not smart."

"Yeah? Huh. I don't have any on me either. But I'm gonna go get some here in a little bit."

He walked over to the side with his buddy and said, "Hey, you know? Forget the weed, why don't we go get some cocaine here in a bit."

Nosferatu said, "Yeah, absolutely."

Shawn walked over to join them, trying to be discrete, "Hey, where are you going? I might be interested."

Nosferatu looked at Rog. He stepped back. He seemed to be taken off-guard by Shawn's approach. Rog walked to the other side of the table, examining his choice of shots. The conversation went back to the game.

Shawn lost the game, so he went back to the bar with Jerry. He caught Shawn up with what was happening in the Reds game. Rog and his partner went on playing each other.

"I'm gonna put in to play again. Want to play the winner? Shawn asked Jerry.

"Sorry, not my game, man."

After a few games back and forth. Rog asked, "You still interested in that white?"

"Yeah, absolutely, I am."

"Well, we can take you on down the road. *Trent*," nodding to his buddy, "just called our guy, he's on."

Shawn nodded. He knew it meant the trafficker had his supply there.

"What do you want?" asked Rog.

"Well, I'll probably get a gram or two. How much?"

Rog shrugged. "I don't know. We'll go down there and see how much he'll charge."

"Why don't you call him back and see how much he wants for it?"

"Nah, we'll go down. We'll work out a good deal for you."

Rog looked at his friend, now identified as *Trent*, and nodded again. Trent nodded back.

Shawn felt uneasy about this. Usually, as an undercover, he liked to know how much upfront. It's like anything else. You want to know how much you'll be paying. Shawn was an aggressive undercover cop, so he let it go.

"When do you want to go?

Shawn stepped forward and looked at his watch. "Let's go now if you want. I've got to go pick up my kid from my x-mother-in-law, who's babysitting. So, I'm running out of time here."

Shawn walked up to Jerry to let him know that he was going to go with Rog and Trent to pick up some white. Today, with all the precautions in place, Jerry wouldn't have stayed at the bar. They would have set a backup plan in place. During this time, however, it was cowboying up. The undercover cops did what they had to do to find out information.

Rog had called his supplier and said they were on their way. Shawn drove with Trent in the back seat behind him and Rog riding shotgun. When they arrived, Trent stayed in the car with Shawn, while Rog walked down to an impressive, well-kept old house. Rog had been careful to make Shawn park seven houses down, but it was easy for Shawn to see where he went. Rog said he was going to go into the house first to find out how much the guy was charging, and that he was going to get some too.

When he returned, Rog said, "He's going to charge you a hundred twenty dollars for a gram, and he'll give you a deal for two grams for two hundred."

"That's pretty steep," said Shawn. "Why don't we make it two grams for a hundred eighty?"

Rog leaned into the car. "Man, this guy...it's what it is."

Shawn took out his wallet and gave Rog a hundred twenty dollars. Rog went back to the house to make the deal. No problems. When he returned to the car and sat down, Shawn turned to him and said, "Hey Rog, let's see the dope."

Rog said, "I got it. We'll square up when we get back to the bar."

Shawn felt a red flag go up. Why wasn't Rog giving him his cocaine? Shawn reflected on two against one. Trent was sitting directly behind him; he could see him in the rearview mirror. Shawn merely put the car in gear. His hair was standing up on the back of his neck. Since there was no back-up, he decided to back off and play it cool. "Okay, dude. We'll work it out when we get back to the Keg Room."

Minutes later, they pulled into the parking lot and strode back into the bar. Shawn nodded to Jerry, who looked at him with eyebrows raised. Shawn put out both hands, palms down to let him know everything was fine.

Rog walked to Shawn and said, "Let's go into the bathroom."

The dimly lit bathroom stunk. The urinal was an old trench. Next to it was a toilet in a doorless stall. It was overflowing with urine, feces, and vomit. The stench made Shawn's eyes water, and he had to concentrate on controlling his gag reflex. Shawn rubbed his nose, trying to hold his breath. Rog stared at him. His right hand held the bag of white. "You're gonna give me some of this, aren't you?"

Shawn said, "I thought you got your own!"

"Nah, man. I didn't have enough cash on me. So, give me a little bump of what you got."

"No, dude. I'm gonna need all this tonight. Me and my girl is gonna party! I ain't giving you any of it."

Rog stared at Shawn. His face was getting red, and his eyes were squinting. His hand was forming a fist. "Look, dude. I went outta my way. I don't know you. You could be a cop for all I know. I hooked you up," gesturing with the bag, "I deserve a bump of this."

"Look, dude. You shoulda told me. I would've given you a couple of bucks to get some for yourself." Shawn knew he had to be careful. The way the law was written for undercover cops if he gave Rog some of the coke, it was considered a "reversal." He needed to have prior approval by the prosecutor's office to do that maneuver. His saving grace was there was a provision that if the officer's safety or someone else's safety was at risk, the officer was allowed to give back some of the drugs to preserve the integrity of the case or the security of the officer.

At this point, Rog said, "Look. I'm getting some of this."

He pulled up his shirt to let Shawn see a gun stuck in his pants. At this point, Shawn knew he had to appease him.

Shawn put his hands on his hips. "Okay, dude. Take a little bit."

Rog lowered his shirt and said, "Okay, man. I don't trust you. We're gonna do it together. I think you're a cop."

"Dude. I'm not doing any of this right here."

"Yeah, you are."

Rog took his forearm and rubbed it across the scummy toilet bowl lid. He skimmed off the urine, feces, and vomit with his swipe. He lined what Shawn thought was a quarter of the gram of coke in two lines. Rog straightened up and said, "You go first."

"I'm not snorting cocaine off of that filthy, nasty toilet lid!"

"Well, okay. Then I'm gonna do both lines."

"Okay, if you do. You owe me money!"

Rog just grinned. "Well, dude. I'll hook you up again next time."

All Shawn could do was a shrug. "All right."

Rog then bent over and snorted both lines of cocaine off the toilet lid, along with the other stuff festering there.

Once he was done, Rog snapped straight like he had a tight spring in his spine. He screamed, "Shit, that was fucking rocket fuel."

Shawn knew the whole bar must have heard him. He stuck out his hand. After a long pause, Rog put the rest of the white in it. Shawn could see now only half of his package was left.

Shawn grinned at him and pointed to his chest. "Look, man.

You owe me. You took half of it. My girl and I were going to party. Now we don't have a lot to party with!"

"Dude, ya shoulda done it with me!"

Shawn stuck to his cover story. "I can't. I gotta pick up my kid. My x-mother-in-law knows I use. I can't pick up my kid high. She'd tell my x, and things would get fucked up, man."

"Okay, okay. Next time we get together, I'll do you right."

Shawn left the restroom and took a breath. He walked up to the bar, straddled a bar stool, and sat down next to Jerry. He put both arms up on the bar and put his hand up and ran it through his hair.

"God, you smell bad!" said Jerry.

Shawn sighed and nodded. Jerry nodded toward the pool table. "He's happy."

Shawn looked over his shoulder to see Rog playing pool. He was louder than ever and jumping around, trying trick shots. After watching Rog almost fall on his face, Jerry said, "Looks like it was some quality stuff."

As they paid their tab and got ready to walk out, Rog came up to Shawn and put his hand on his shoulder. Rog told Jerry how cool Shawn was, what a great guy he was.

Jerry smiled and said, "Yeah, I know all that, but this great guy better drive home with the windows down."

Suddenly, Rog stopped. His eyes glazed over. He ran out to the patio and vomited over the side. He stumbled back in and yelled, "Man, that was fuckin' rocket fuel!"

Everybody now in the place looked up, saw it was Rog and laughed. Jerry said, "Looks like this might be an everyday thing for ol' Rog."

Jerry and Shawn left the bar.

After some research, Shawn was able to identify Rog through his first name, his tats, and even where he lived. He found Rog had a long history of juvenile crime, domestic violence, robbery, and gun violations. Shawn, with the blessing of his supervisors, decided to continue the investigation. There was a trafficker to go after. He called the number Rog gave him but didn't get an answer. He and Jerry decided to return the Keg Room the next Friday to try and hook up with him again.

Rog wasn't there. They sat down at the bar and asked the bartender if she knew where he was.

"Rog won't be in here for a while."

"Why?"

"He shot a guy."

It turns out the Saturday after they had met Rog, he argued with another patron and shot the guy in the leg and stomach. The guy survived, but Rog ended up in prison for felonious assault. The investigation of the house continued ending with several arrests and confiscation of several grams of cocaine and bags of marijuana. Further work took years to apprehend the more significant supplier. Ironically, it was Rog, who was a substantial informer for Shawn and Jerry. After his release for good behavior, they managed to apprehend him on a drug possession charge. To work off some of the time on that charge, he worked with the sheriff's department, giving them pieces of information that would allow them to gather evidence to locate where the drugs were emanating.

PART FIVE

Michael 1989

The Cartel

Spring of 1989

Mike was working undercover in East Columbus when he received a phone message to call Sheriff Bob McArthur in Fayette County.

"Mike, you won't believe who we have in custody. An old friend of yours."

"Hey, Bob, who?"

"Kyle Safford."

"You're kidding me."

"Nope. Right here in the flesh."

"I didn't know he was even out!"

"He's out, alright. Hope you're sitting down. He wants to work with law enforcement."

"You're shittin' me. How'd this come about?"

The Fayette County Sheriff's Department had executed a search warrant for Ray Littell. Inside his house, they encountered Rena and Kyle Safford. Rena was Ray's live-in girlfriend, and Kyle had just gotten out of prison. The sheriff's department had been watching Littell for quite some time. Executing the search warrant, they came across an eighth of an ounce of cocaine (about the size of a pack of Sweet and Lo ®). Kyle told the deputies who were there, it was his. Not Rena's or Ray's.

"When Robinson and I walked into the interview room, the deputy told me Safford wanted to work with law enforcement. You remember Washington Courthouse Police Chief Robinson?"

"Of course."

"I was so surprised. I wasn't sure I heard him right."

Mike laughed.

"I asked Kyle to tell me."

He said, "I'll work with law enforcement."

"I told him fine. We can do that. But I was going to tell him it'll be contingent on what he gave us when he interrupted me."

"He said, 'But there's only one guy I'll work with.'"

"And he said me."

"Yup."

"I'll be damned."

"Both the chief and I are a little suspicious, but... I had to give you a call."

Like the sheriff and police chief, Mike wondered if he was being set up. He and Kyle had been through a lot, and it gave Mike gooseflesh to think where this might lead. Mike knew Safford had connections all over the United States. But he also knew how dangerous Safford could be.

Mike went to his superiors and told them what he knew. He garnered permission to go two counties away, but everyone he spoke to warned him about the danger of working with Safford.

The risk was real. If Mike worked with Safford, Safford could pull a gun on him or double-cross him and set him up. Mike remembered the look on Safford's face as he was being led away after being convicted. Mike knew he was taking a chance. On his way down to Washington Courthouse that night, Mike felt a mixture of anticipation and fear. He hoped, like other criminals he had worked with, Safford realized what kind of life he would have if he continued to be in and out of prison. Safford was still young and could turn his life around.

Mike let the sheriff know he was on his way. Mike was met by a plainclothesman outside of town. Everyone wanted to take precautions just in case Mike was going undercover again to work with Kyle.

When Mike entered the interview room, he scrutinized Kyle. The hatred and meanness were gone. Kyle's face lit up when he saw Mike. His shoulders drew up and then down as Kyle took a breath of relief. Right then, Mike knew Kyle would be open and honest with him. Mike asked the deputy to take the handcuffs off Kyle. As the deputy unlocked Kyle's right hand, Mike extended his hand. Kyle stood and took it in a firm grip. Mike then asked if he and Kyle could talk alone.

Mike told Kyle what the sheriff had said that brought him down to Fayette County. "Kyle, I don't understand. Why did you want to talk to me?"

"Like I told the sheriff. I'm tired of going to prison. I don't' want to risk it anymore. I'm taking this dope on my back because I don't want my sister in any more trouble. I don't want her boyfriend in trouble; Ray's trying to get his life together. I want them to have a chance. Mike, you know I've never worked with law enforcement. They've always treated me bad. But I knew there was one officer I could trust. And that officer was you."

Pausing, Mike leaned his hand on his chin with his fingers covering his mouth and looked at Kyle. Taking his hand away, he smiled. "How do you know you can trust me?"

Kyle's eyes, emphasized by his thick glasses, were intense. "Because when I went to trial, I sat and watched you as you testified. I knew every word you said was true. Even though I didn't want to hear it, I did every damn word you said. Rena did. And Gene did. All of it was true. All that was the-honest-to-God truth. There was no lying. You blew nothing up. So, I felt I could trust you. That's what I'm doing now."

Mike went through the complicated procedures to have permission from the sheriff's department, probation, and the parole board to work with Kyle. He knew the charge against Kyle was pending, and whatever he did for law enforcement would earn him consideration. Even though he was arrested, he would not be indicted for the drug charge yet. The prosecutor could hold the case or dismiss it. Kyle had to provide work that would satisfy Mike and the other agencies.

After Kyle's release, he and Mike would spend a lot of time together in Kyle's new place on the outskirts of Washington Courthouse. Mike had to go only at night and wear a ball cap to disguise himself. Or he would pick up Kyle and take him to downtown Columbus. They constructed Mike's cover story that Kyle would use when he introduced Mike to his contacts. Kyle had met Shawn James Edwards (Mike) in prison. "Eddie" was from Toledo, Lucas County, Ohio. Eddie had lost his connection in Toledo for cocaine and other drugs. Now he had to make different connections. Kyle had told him he would help him do that when they got out. Mike got a Lucas County address for his driver's license. It was an actual license arranged through the BMV, so the police officers would know he was legal if stopped.

They spent hours talking about what Kyle had been through, who he knew, and what amounts each of his connections could get. Mike would listen. Kyle had been in prison for seven years for the drug charges he was convicted on through Mike's work in 1981. Now he had to reconnect with his contacts, plus introduce his buddy "Eddie."

Kyle had to learn what he could and couldn't do while working with law enforcement. They had to discuss the legal definition of entrapment and what actions it would entail. He or Mike couldn't trick or suggest to a person to take a drug or money to cause someone to break the law to be arrested. They needed to talk about how they would communicate with each other if a confrontation occurred. Kyle needed to learn that the dealer could give only Mike the drugs, and only Mike could give or take money. If Kyle did those things, he could be called into court to testify, and no one wanted that to happen. It would make him a target. They wanted to keep Kyle safe from any retaliation to live his life after this was all over. He had to be clear that his job was to get Mike through the door, but only Mike needed to do the talking to seal the deal. Kyle could not be around any drugs or weapons unless Mike was present or had given him permission to carry. Then there was more paperwork to be filled out for him to work as an informant for law enforcement. The plan took days and days of them working together for both to feel secure in making this work.

Kyle's incentive was to ensure no charges were filed on him or Rena. Rena wouldn't know Kyle was working with Mike. Mike could not work with Kyle within Washington Courthouse, so their undercover work would not be exposed by anyone who would remember Mike.

JJ Lesko was the first significant user of cocaine they approached. JJ injected cocaine regularly. He didn't even question when Kyle brought Mike around. Living in Hillsboro, Ohio, he had a serious connection in Chillicothe by the name of *Ty Jameson*. Kyle knew JJ, but not his connection. Their first buy would entail picking up Lesko and taking him to see Jameson. Jameson would take the money, get the cocaine, and get it back to Mike. They would provide Lesko with a small amount of cocaine for setting up the transaction. Mike had to go to the prosecutor beforehand with the details and get permission to give Lesko the cocaine.

Heading down to Hillsboro, Mike was preparing himself for a similar experience he had in Washington Courthouse. Hillsboro is a small city with 6,300 people and only about 2,600 households. Ninety percent of the people were white, with an average income of approximately $26,000 a year. Similar to Washington Courthouse, everybody knew everybody. The significant difference for Mike was Kyle. He was relying on him to make it simple for him.

Kyle and Mike pulled up to a duplex. They walked up the steps, and JJ answered the door. Mike was struck by JJ's gaunt appearance. His drawn face was almost skeletal. His setback eyes and wide pupils signaled Mike JJ was using. Once inside, Mike wanted to recoil from his loose, bony handshake. Behind JJ, sitting on a filthy carpet, was a little seven-year-old kid playing with a set of Legos. ™ As they stepped into the living room, Mike smelled a faint odor, like a mixture of weed and garbage. Clothes were strewn on the furniture. At a quick glance, the coffee table and side tables were covered with takeout boxes and stuff.

Kyle told JJ, "Eddie here wants to buy an ounce of coke."

JJ turned his head to look at Mike. "That'll be no problem. We'll have to run over to Ty's. It'll run you about $1,200 for that ounce."

Mike said, "I can get the money."

"No, no." JJ, gesturing with a waving hand, "There won't be any *getting* the money. You gotta *have* the money. No getting the money. You gotta have it."

"I got the money."

Mike could see how rubber band-tight JJ was. Mike knew his whole being was dedicated to making himself feel good.

JJ called someone to come look after the kid. As they were waiting, Mike went to the bathroom. He found a ringed scummy tub and sink still showing remnants from a morning shave. By the sink juxtaposed to each other was a little kid's toothbrush with Sesame Street's Elmo™ brightly smiling and an uncapped insulin one hundred syringe with a bit of dried blood on the tip. When he needed to wash his hands, he didn't want to touch the handles of the sink's faucet. He leaned down and washed his hands, using the tap in the bathtub. Yellowish towels hung askew on their racks, so Mike wiped his hands on his pants.

As he returned to the front room, JJ said, "Wait a minute. I left my pointer in the bathroom!"

It took about forty-five minutes to an hour to make their way to Chillicothe through the scenery of open land, hills, and farmhouses. JJ was in the backseat while Kyle sat in front with Mike. For the entire ride, JJ talked. He's got great connects. Big ones. His connects go straight to the cartel. Mike kept thinking, *yeah, sure. That's what they all like you to believe. He's full of shit. They all say they are going to get you the best dope you've ever had.*

They planned to have JJ introduce Kyle to Ty and soon work JJ out of the deal. In contrast, JJ's idea was to stay connected to them so he could supply his habit.

Finally, they arrived at a small white house with bright blue shuttered windows. JJ knocked on the door. On the other side, Mike heard a growl. "Yeah, who is it?"

When JJ answered, the door opened. A bald black man in his late forties, about five foot eight and four hundred pounds, filled the doorway. As the man moved away, he shook hands with JJ and gave him a half-bro hug. He addressed Kyle with, "I heard you got out."

"Yeah, here's Eddie. I work with him."

As *Ty* moved forward to shake his hand, Mike had to fight the urge to step back.

"You the man who wants the O?"

"Yeah."

"Well, we have a trip."

"Yeah, where?"

"Columbus."

"I'm not familiar. You'll have to direct me."

"No problem. We'll be traveling to the north end."

Mike shrugged with one shoulder. "Okay, cool."

Mike had dressed for this meet in worn jeans and a cutoff sweatshirt. His hair was covered with a bandana, but he was still concerned because they were returning to Franklin County, where more people knew him. What if someone recognized him and blew the entire operation? He was also laser aware he had $1,200 on him. That was a lot of money for Mike, and his nervousness put him even more in jeopardy. Mike had set up surveillance with five cars backing them up, but somehow that knowledge did not set his mind at ease.

Ty sat in the front with Mike. For the whole forty-eight minutes to Columbus, Ty peppered Mike with questions. He first started with Mike's experiences in prison. "What were you in for? How long? When did you get out?" He tried to ask about personal matters, such as if he had a woman? Who does "Eddie" sell the coke to? How does he operate to stay away from the police? Finally, Ty directed Mike to Genesis Avenue in the Short North District. He told him to park on a short side road.

Ty stuck out his hand, almost taking Mike off guard, and said, "I need the money."

Mike put his hand on the lever to open the car. Ty barked to stay where he was. Mike braced his feet on the floorboards and dug the $1,200 out of his jeans pocket. He gave it to him. Ty said, "Don't get out of the car."

The car sagged and sprung back as Ty strained to get out of the vehicle. Mike knew he walked down the street they had turned from, but he couldn't gawk or turn to watch where Ty went because JJ was in the back seat. JJ's chatter almost got on Mike's last nerve after forty-five minutes. Thankfully, Ty returned.

Climbing back in the car, Ty said, "Well, let's head back."

Mike asked him, "Did you get the baggage?"

"Yeah, I got the baggage. I'll show you the package when we get back to Chillicothe."

An hour later, they were back at Ty's house. Ty went into the kitchen. Mike followed and saw him take the package out of his inside coat pocket. To Mike, it looked like white powdered sugar with big chunks. The chunks meant high-quality stuff because they came right off the kilo (kilo brick). It seemed to be a two-ounce package. At the bottom was a bit of powder.

Over his shoulder, Ty said, "I'm going to weigh this out."

"It should weigh out at twenty-eight."

"Well, you'll weigh out at twenty-five to twenty-eight cuz I'm going to take a little pinch, and JJ here is gonna take a little pinch."

Mike was already thinking about how he's going to explain how much they were going to take. Ty did what he said, and the package weighed twenty-five grams when they were finished. Kyle and Mike thanked Ty and got back in the car to take JJ back to Hillsboro.

After a twelve-hour day, Mike was back in the property room at the Franklin County Sheriff's Department, recording the buy and doing the required paperwork for the day's work. When Mike went home at 3:30 AM and fell into bed, he felt good about the day and the transaction.

Kyle, Mike, and JJ would return to the little white bright blue shuttered house in Chillicothe often for minor transactions with Ty. Mike wanted to ensure Ty knew them enough to cut JJ out of their dealings. Mike was concerned because Ty was taking really stupid risks that could cause the local police to come and cut off their connection to Columbus.

One evening, Kyle and Mike arrived at Ty's door without JJ to see what would happen. Mike knocked on the front door. Again, they heard, "Who is it?"

Kyle said, "It's Kyle and Eddie."

The door swung open. Ty yelled, "Come on in."

Ty was in an aggressive position as they came in, like a defensive tackle coming off the line. "Who in the fuck are you two to come here without JJ? What the fuck do you think you're doin' without him?"

Mike, remembering his gun was in the car, was on his toes, ready to move if he had to. He stood with his hands out. "I'm gonna be honest with you, Ty. Uh, you know JJ. The problem is I wanna make some money, and so does Kyle. Me going through JJ., I've gotta give him some. You're cutting the package too. You know my package is light. I'm not makin' the money I need to make. Then I gotta transport that dope back to Toledo and resell it. It's a pain. Dude, you want ta yell at me. You don't trust me. You think I'm the po-lice, or Kyle is. You do what ya gotta do." Mike gestured with his thumb. "If you want us to get the fuck out of your place, we'll get the fuck outta here."

Mike motioned for Kyle to leave. Kyle seemed frozen in place, his eyes wide and his face ashen.

There was a pause.

"Okay, okay, stop." Ty relaxed his aggressive stance. "Wait, you know I gotta ask. You don't know who you can trust anymore."

Taking a big breath, Kyle extended his hand. "You know me, man. I'm not going to do anything stupid."

Ty said, "Okay, how much do you want?"

Mike said, "Another ounce. If you can get me the same ounce."

"Let me make a phone call."

Ty left the room. When he returned, he said, "Hey, two boys are coming over with a package. It's here in town. They just have to run and pick it up."

Mike had the impression they would have to fetch the package, but twenty minutes later, two rough, scrawny guys came walking into Ty's house. Mike thought they looked like two basketball players standing in Ty's tidy living room. Ty turned to Mike with a nod toward the two guys and said, "You got the money? Dude, you need twelve."

Mike was stuck. He realized he was supposed to hand these two over the $1,200. They would take the money, and he was supposed to trust they would return with cocaine. He wouldn't know where they had gone or who they had contacted. The surveillance team wouldn't realize to follow them because they didn't know what was happening in the house. Neither Mike nor Kyle was wearing a body wire.

Mike ended up giving the money to Ty, and Ty gave the money to the two guys. Without a word, the two left the house. Mike stewed and paced for an hour until they came back. To make the time even slower, Mike had to listen to Ty talk about his experiences in the penitentiary, how he didn't want to go back, and what a valuable asset Ty was to them. It was clear to Mike that he was jonesing for some cocaine. Ty also kept babbling about one of his connections being down and how things weren't happening. Mike thought he might be talking about the Columbus connection.

Sitting on the couch waiting, Kyle jumped when the front door swung open. Mike stood. The two guys walked straight to Ty and handed him a plastic bag of powder. Mike saw it contained very little rock, so he knew it would not be the same quality cocaine. From the wide-eyed, happy-go-lucky jabber of the two guys, Mike knew they had already taken some of the cocaine for themselves. Ty went straight to the kitchen to measure out his "pinch." When Mike received the package, he estimated it would be less than twenty-five grams.

After the cocaine was tested in the forensic lab, it proved Mike right. The twenty-five grams were not the quality of the cocaine they had received in Columbus.

Mike told his supervisors he wanted to return to Ty's house early in the day, maybe nine or ten in the morning. Ty's wife worked long hours at Adena Regional Medical Center, and she would be gone from the residence. He wanted to find Ty alone. He would give Ty a sob story about having to make more money. Mike had to hope Ty wouldn't be high. He needed to drive his wife to work, so the earlier hour would be a safer bet. The supervisors approved, and they went about setting surveillance for Mike's safety.

A week later, Mike knocked on Ty's door at 8:30 a.m. morning, saying, "Hey, Ty. It's Eddie."

Ty opened the door, smiling." Hey, Eddie. How are ya doing? Haven't seen you for a while."

"Look, if you have a couple of minutes, I'm in a bind. I've gotta make some money. I got a situation up in Toledo. Kyle told me he had to work today, so I decided that I'd just come to see you alone. I hope you don't mind. I need a package. A quality two-ounce package where I can make some good money. I'm reaching out to you and anyone else I can. I gotta have by the weekend."

"Okay. That gives me two days. Cool, my girl's on. You want to do it tomorrow?"

"Can you do it tomorrow?" Mike was surprised, but really excited.

"Yeah. I can do it tomorrow morning. I got to take my old lady to work. Then I'm good to go. I don't want to take my car up there. Can you drive?"

"Yeah."

"Meet me here about nine. We'll go."

The next day, Mike was nervous. He was carrying $2,400 to buy two ounces of coke. The department had five cars running surveillance for him again. He had instructed the men to not follow closely, but if they lose him, he told them he thought he could handle Ty. Mike hid a gun under the front seat. He seldom carried a gun in these situations unless he picked up indicators it was dangerous. Here, it was a smart thing to do. He was going to Columbus carrying a lot of money to meet with individuals who were unknown to him.

As they neared the Genesee area, Ty wanted to stop at a payphone. In 1989, pay phones were still easy to find. Mike opened his window to catch some conversation. He heard Ty say, "Damn!"

Mike immediately felt deflated. Nothing was going to happen, and he had that $2,400 on him. Ty came back rocking the car as he got in. "She doesn't have the package yet."

"Is she going to have it today?"

Ty shrugged. "She wasn't sure. Hey, I can call around to other connects and see what they have."

"Hey, I gotta client who wants that high-quality snow. I can't make the same amount of money, and this client won't be happy. Should we wait around? Come back tomorrow? What do you think?" Mike realized his volume was raised along with his pitch.

Ty turned and leaned against the door. Taking Mike in, he shrugged again. "I don't know, man. Let's drive around a bit. Give her some time to assess."

They drove around the Short North neighborhoods and on the freeways. Mike kept talking about how Columbus differs from Toledo. Ty was quiet, only commenting about the size of the city. Mike kept seeing the same cars, knowing they were his guys. He hoped Ty wouldn't notice. He went through the downtown area of Columbus, trying to lose the surveillance team before Ty caught on to what was happening.

After four hours of driving, they took a pit stop, and Ty called again. Ty punched in the phone number and watched Mike as he talked. Mike saw Ty's face break out in a smile. Guiding his balk back into the car, he said, "We're on Eddie!"

"Thank God."

Mike guided the car back down the main roads and side streets to the Genesee Avenue area. Ty motioned to Mike to parallel park in front of a little blue house. Once parked, Ty turned and stuck out his hand. "Eddie, give me the money."

Mike reached inside his jacket and gave it to him. Ty took out a piece of paper from his pocket. He wrapped the money in the paper and placed it under his ball cap. Opening the car door, Ty swung one leg out at a time. He then grabbed the door frame and pulled himself upright. Mike watched as Ty climbed three cement steps using a white rail to assist him. Looking around a bit, Ty went up the sidewalk to the front steps of the house. Knocking, the door opened, but Mike couldn't see the person who opened it.

Mike shifted after waiting for twenty minutes. After cruising around for so long, he wanted to stretch his legs. Hearing a car, he glanced up and saw a powder blue Corvette coming down the street. He watched it pass him, noting the dealer tags. In his outside rearview mirror, he saw it turn around and park a few car lengths behind him. Watching a blonde woman dressed in an executive-like black suit and heels exit the car, he watched as she walked up the street carrying a briefcase. She walked right by his driver's side and turned in front of his car to go up the same steps Ty had climbed before.

Mike was floored. Could this be the woman Ty was dealing with? If she was, she certainly looked well-to-do and well connected. Mike opened the glove compartment and took out a small pad and pen to write the dealer tag numbers.

Minutes later, Ty came back out and down the stairs. As he opened the door and maneuvered back into the car, Mike had a feeling he was high.

"Dude, that took a while!"

"Yeah, yeah, yeah! There were no problems..."

"Yeah, but did you get it?"

"Yeah!" Ty took his ball cap off and took out a baggie of cocaine.

Mike had seen nothing like it. It looked as if they had just cut it off a cocaine loaf. "Dude, I've never seen anything like that."

"Yeah, my girl. She just came over."

"Yeah, I saw some well-heeled bitch go up there, man! Carrying a briefcase."

"Yeah, that's my girl. Her name is *Miriam*. She opened that case in the kitchen. They took out a knife, and she started cutting pieces off. We weighed off two just for you."

Mike showed his excitement to match Ty's, but his excitement was for entirely different reasons. Mike knew whoever Miriam was; she was one very serious connection.

The ride back was the longest drive Mike had ever experienced. Ty had the cocaine under his cap, and Mike needed to find a pay phone to call into the office. As soon as he dropped Ty off, he found a phone and called into headquarters. He knew who ever lived in that house was part of a bigger picture, perhaps a small part, but definitely a part of a huge connection. Mike wanted to get a quiet search warrant, maybe five or six hours after they had done their transaction. Whatever was left of the kilo was up at the Genesee location. Whoever lived at that location had a direct connection to this Miriam in the powder blue Corvette. He didn't want a dramatic SWAT team blowing the doors off the place. He didn't wish for Miriam to know she couldn't make that contact on Genesee anymore.

As soon as Mike got back to the office, he arranged for the search warrant. He set up a team to do reconnaissance to let him know if there was any traffic coming or going at the house. His team let him know there was only minor traffic now. Mike knew there would be less cocaine there, but he also knew some of the pre-recorded bills of $2,400 would be there.

Mike ran the dealer tag on the powder blue Corvette while he waited. It went back to a car repair shop, Jack McCall's Repair Shop, on Cleveland Avenue. Mike sent a team up to that general area to look for the Corvette. They couldn't locate it.

The unit executed the quiet search warrant at the little blue house on Genesee Avenue. The search warrant reaped a half-ounce of cocaine and about one hundred eighty dollars of the pre-recorded money, along with a handgun. Living at the house was *Peg Reinitz*.

Mike's job now was to interrogate her. When he came into the small, bare room, Peg was quiet. Mike introduced himself and told her the Sheriff's Drug Force had been conducting surveillance at her location for a few days. He created a story for her of watching a black Cadillac pull up in front of her house with a white male driving and a large black man getting out and going up to her place. A woman opened the front door and let him enter. As the white male waited, a female then drove up. She came out of a powder blue Corvette, carrying a briefcase. The surveillance team then said the black man and his driver left, and soon after, so did the woman in the Corvette.

Peg said, "Yeah, that was me. I let the guy in. The guy you saw was Ty Jackson. He lives in Chillicothe. He brought some guy down, but the guy didn't come in, so I have no idea who it was. I called Miriam. She lives in Gahanna. Her name is *Miriam McCall*. She brought the kilo over, and we cut it up. I gave some to Ty, and he left."

Peg was a smart woman. She was a single mother who had a young daughter living with her. Mike knew she didn't want to go to jail and make her daughter go into the system. He arranged with the prosecutor to keep her out of jail if she cooperated to help indict Miriam.

Mike had previously arranged with the Ross County Sheriff and the Chillicothe police to have an arrest warrant for Ty issued. Mike was concerned that once Peg, his connection in Columbus, went down, he would receive a phone call and realize that Mike, who was known as Eddie, was responsible.

Ty had told Mike several times he did not want to go back to prison. Mike wasn't surprised when he got a call from Ross County law enforcement that Ty would cooperate with them. Fortunately, Ty did not realize Mike was an undercover detective. He assumed surveillance had "Eddie" arrested, too.

Peg's Story

With tape and videotape recorders running plus other law enforcement watching, Peg told her story. Most of the time, she talked with her hands folded in front of her. Any other time, she held a Styrofoam cup between her hands. Her face expressionless as if she was reciting.

Miriam McCoy had direct connections to some significant cocaine cartel members from Columbia. They ran their operation out of Florida and New York City but did business in cities across the United States. She had two girls who lived with her at her residence in Gahanna. The two girls were former strippers from local joints in Columbus. These two strippers, who were in their mid-twenties, met two Columbian men when they frequented their club. These two men would drop big money to spend time with them. The men's goal was to find young women who had a legal driver's license. The women were recruited to drive doctored cars purchased by the Columbia cartel.

The cartels financed airfare for the girls to fly down to Miami. They were put up in nice motels and given money for gas and expenses. They would then drive back in the doctored cars, now containing a substantial amount of cocaine hidden in secret compartments. Warned never to look for the compartments, the girls were to pretend they were coming back from a vacation down in Florida.

Once the girls returned to Columbus, they called an 800 number. Other cartel members here in Columbus would pick up the vehicles from the Gahanna location and take the autos to the Jack McCall Auto Shop or other similar places. At these places, they would open the secret compartments and take out the kilos of cocaine. Hundreds of thousands of dollars would replace the cocaine in the secret compartments. The girls received a phone call, given the keys to the readied and newly secured cars, and given instructions to drive the car back to Florida, or New York City to the Bronx or Queens area. The money would be recycled and replaced by more kilos.

All this information was recorded, but now it had to be confirmed. Miriam and her ex-husband, *Jack McCoy*, had teams of surveillance assigned to them. From there, it was easy to find out the names of the strippers, now transporters.

Nine County Investigation

The investigation expanded to a nine-county, five-city task force and covered Franklin, Pickaway, Ross, Pike, Scioto, Fayette, Adams, Brown, and Clinton Counties. Included were smaller cities of Portsmouth, Washington Court House, Wilmington, Chillicothe, and Waverly. Mike was now supervising a task force that had increased to nineteen officers working simultaneously covering these areas. To allow the operation to be more centralized, the offices were at Rickenbacker Air National Guard Base.

Every week Mike ran a large briefing for all Sheriffs and Chiefs from each jurisdiction to communicate what had been accomplished in each of their areas the previous week. Any agency that joined the Task Force chose the officers they thought would be best for the assignment. Rigorous training was provided for the officers. Each officer had to go through a week of training on paperwork to complete offense reports and impound sheets. All funds had to be signed for and all expenditures required reports, and expense cards had to be completed. Every officer was required to keep a complete record of his funds received and spent as did the supervisors. Other training that needed to be completed covered ethics and entrapment. The new undercover officers had to complete the course that Mike had created for the State of Ohio earlier in his career. They were then assigned to an experienced officer to guide them, so they became more aware of the different types of police work outside of the type of work when wearing a uniform. After completing the training, some officers decided undercover wasn't what they thought and returned to their previous assignments.

This was a difficult assignment for Mike since he was responsible for all the undercover buys for each jurisdiction. Each area provided funds for the operations they ran. Luckily, another supervisor was responsible for money management.

Mike had daily roll calls with the agents to relate their achievements or discuss what they had to do next. He ended each of his roll calls with reminding them that mistakes could be deadly. Besides supervising these investigations, he was also involved in some of the transactions himself. All the officers were supposed to work only forty-hour weeks, but sometimes, as in the case of Mike, opportunities or problems came up. Overtime was limited. Occasionally, comp time became available for officers, but rarely.

The challenges were daily and only became more complex when one of his own officers found himself in trouble. *Terry Stanford* was a Franklin County deputy sheriff. Stanford was chosen out of the twenty-five applicants. He had excellent communication skills and was skilled as an undercover narcotics officer. Mike thought Stanford would manage any occasion he would have to face. He had the knowledge to talk street dope, and he could handle the freedom and temptations involved to receive money to buy drugs or work a bar or other settings he would encounter. He'd act the part of purchasing drug paraphernalia and put it in his undercover car to give the appearance *he was cool.* This was a phrase used by big-time dealers and small-time operators. A small thing like this was essential to not let on that he was a cop. He exhibited the discipline to go into bars where the Sheriff's Office had received complaints of drug abuse and trafficking and consume small amounts of alcohol.

Stanford went through rigorous undercover training and performed well. His only flaw was that he wasn't good with paperwork, but that was an easy fix. After about a year, Stanford was teamed with a more experienced officer to investigate a bar in a very rough section of the county that reportedly was dealing in weed, cocaine, crack, and pills.

In a few weeks, Stanford started making a few small deals with individuals in the bar. He brought back small amounts of weed initially and then grams amounts of crack cocaine. Gradually, he was working on other complaints in the Chillicothe area. Sometimes he was working with an informant, other times he met on his own with a dealer. Stanford was showing an ability to fit into any crowd. His confidence allowed a dealer to trust him.

Within a few months, he started to be a little late coming into the office. When Mike talked to him, Stanford blamed it on not being able to sleep. He was also having some domestic problems. Not sleeping well because of shift changes was a common problem in this field. Stanford had a wife and two kids, so adjusting to his new schedule and the job demands were common.

A week or two after Mike talked to him, Stanford had another incident. He said he came home late one night after work, and he locked his gun in his undercover car. During the night, someone broke into the vehicle and stole his weapon. They did a report on the stolen firearm, and he was issued another one from the county. During that same period, another agent, *Andy Blackwell,* came to Mike. He said he had misplaced two hundred dollars of buy money. Blackwell wasn't sure how it happened because he always kept his cash in a locked briefcase until he was ready to use it. The amount he had wasn't unusual. Most undercovers carried two hundred fifty dollars to five hundred dollars for deals and expenses. Mike told him he was responsible for the money and would have to replace the amount if he didn't locate the lost funds. Blackwell asked Mike, "Do you think somebody in the office would have taken it?"

Surprised, Mike replied, "I think everyone in the unit is pretty trustworthy."

Blackwell took two hundred dollars from his personal account and gave it to the other supervisor to make up for the loss.

For a few months, no other problems were reported, until one afternoon Stanford came up to Mac about 4 p.m. (Officer's hours varied according to shifts. Stanford was working 4 p.m. to midnight.)

He said he was working a complaint in Chillicothe, and he met a guy who sold him a couple of rocks of crack. He went out to the parking lot and placed the crack in the door handle of his vehicle and returned to the bar because he wanted to try and buy from another person. When he returned to his car, he unlocked his car and found the rocks of crack gone.

"You mean someone broke into your vehicle?" Mike asked.

Stanford shrugged. "You know Mike?" He passed his hand over his hair. "I think I forgot to lock the car! There wasn't any forced entry."

Mike studied Stanford's worried face. Stanford was about 6'2." He was slouching. His green eyes had lost that sparkle of enthusiasm. "Come on, Terry, let's go into my office."

Mike's office was small. All there was room for was a desk, file cabinets, and a chair for someone else to occupy. Gesturing he said, "Sit, Terry," When they were both settled, he continued. "Terry, this job isn't easy. I understand it has its ups and downs. Is everything okay?"

Stanford slouched in his chair. "Yeah. You're right, it's hard. My wife and I are having problems. She doesn't think I'm around enough. We might end up getting divorced."

Mike nodded. Mike himself had weathered a divorce from his high school sweetheart. "I'm sorry to hear that. Maybe back off a bit. Take some time with her and the kids."

Stanford just nodded, got up, opened the office door, and left. Mike decided to believe him but also called his partner in to talk.

After his talk with Stanford's partner, Mike was unsettled. His partner didn't realize Stanford was doing these buys on his own in Chillicothe. He also hadn't reported his buys in the daily meetings or in reports.

Mike walked back into his office after his weekly meeting with the Sheriffs and Chiefs of the counties and small cities when his phone rang.

"Mike? This is *Penny Stanford*."

"Hi, Penny. What's up?"

"Mike, I'm worried about Terry. Something's wrong."

"Hold on a second, Penny. I want to close the door of my office." Mike closed the door and then picked up a pen and positioned a notepad so he could take notes easily. "Tell me what's going on."

"Mike, you warned all of us these hours would be crazy when he took this job, but he's not coming home some nights." Penny took a long shaky breath. "Is that normal?"

Mike wasn't sure what to say. "Well, no."

"I didn't think so." Penny's voice continued to waver a bit. "When he is home, he really gets agitated with me over nothing. I asked him where he was the other night, and he lied to me when he said he had to work all night on surveillance."

"Are you and the kids all right?"

"The kids are fine."

"Okay, I'll try to bring him in to talk to me to see what's up with him. He's always private about his personal life. But I'll try. "

"Thanks, Mike. I appreciate it."

Stanford was not working surveillance all night. Mike wondered if he was seeing another woman. Mike stood and reread the notepad on his desk. He needed to talk to Terry, but he didn't want to make things worse by confronting him on personal life issues. He really felt bad for the couple and their two kids. But he also expected Stanford to do his job and pull his weight in the unit.

Because of his own schedule between the Franklin County investigation and his personal involvement in the nine-county cases, he didn't have a chance to talk to Stanford. Three weeks later, the safe at the headquarters was broken into. When Mike arrived, he discovered $2,000 were stolen. The safe wasn't forced open. Someone found he had left the combination in his center drawer in case he or one of the other supervisors forgot the combination. Mike was angry. He had believed everyone who worked there could be trusted. There was no forced entry from the outside, but a back door was kicked open from the inside. There was no alarm at the headquarters because it was believed to be secure on the base. Mike's phone rang as he was trying to put all the pieces together. Another supervisor answered and told Mike Terry Stanford had been shot.

Mike took the phone to find out more information. Terry had been shot during a deal. He was at Mount Carmel East Hospital. His condition was serious.

Mike took off for the hospital. When he arrived, he found the waiting room where other officers were gathered. Penny was there with her kids. He walked over her and said he was sorry. She nodded as a doctor came in the room to update her. Terry was out of surgery and would fully recover from his injuries. Penny turned to Mike and hugged him. She asked the doctor if she could see him. The doctor told her Terry would be still under anesthetic, but she could sit with him. Mike told her there were enough policemen there to watch the kids. She smiled and left.

Two days later, Mike entered Terry's hospital room. Terry said to his wife, "Penny, I need to talk to Mike alone. Could you excuse me?"

Mike sat by his bed. Terry was still bruised around his eyes and mouth from the beating he had received. His shoulder was bandaged.

"Mike, I can't lie to you anymore. I fucked up really bad." His green eyes filled with tears.

Mike was quiet and let him find his words.

"I want to tell you the truth, but I don't want to go to prison if I admit what I did."

"Terry, stop talking. I have to call the Sheriff and Chief Deputy. You stop and think if you need a lawyer."

Mike called and told them Stanford was confessing. Mike assumed he was confessing about the break in. Both said they would give him a choice. They would not pursue charges if he would resign, or they would fire him and possibly file charges. Mike went back and told Stanford that if he talked, he wouldn't be charged, but he would lose his job and any benefits he had coming.

Terry nodded. "I met this barmaid at The Rugged Bar. You know the complaint location."

Mike nodded.

He snorted. "She was struggling with crack and weed addiction. She was, you know, sweet. I eventually got to purchase some weed from her. She pressed me to smoke some weed with her. And I thought, what the hell. I smoked with her. I was really having a tough time with Penny. She, her name is Trudy, would listen. She gave me some good advice.

She was hot. I was really low, and she made me feel like I was worth listening to. I ended up sleeping with her. One night I smoked crack with her. It made me light with no problems. I wanted to quit, but I wasn't strong enough."

Terry tried to shift his weight wincing as he did.

"I spent most of my paycheck on her and crack. Mike, my gun wasn't stolen. I sold it to buy for crack. I took the money from Blackwell. I spotted his briefcase open, saw his combination, and stole the money to buy crack to smoke with her. I lied about the crack theft too. The safe? I did that too. I came into the office, found the combination in your drawer, opened the safe, and took the money." He laughed a bit, throwing back his head. "I kicked the back door to make it look like whoever got into the office had to run out the back because security was coming around to check the building."

Mike felt responsible. He liked Terry and enjoyed having him in the unit. Stanford had kept the entire unit in the dark about his struggle, feeling helpless. Mike would take his badge, his ID, his keys to his county vehicle, and his gun. After the investigation into the shooting was over, it turned out Trudy told her dealer about Terry. When Terry went to buy crack from the dealer, the dealer thought he was buying the crack to arrest him. He had his men beat Terry and shoot him. Luckily, Trudy had been waiting in the car and heard the gunshot. She called 911.

Mike drove him home from the hospital. He kept thinking about how there something had been special about Terry Stanford. He was so easy to like and had a presence about him. The memory of what happened with Stanford stayed with him for a long time. Just a dumb mistake almost killed him.

Miriam

The next part of Mike' s plan in Franklin County was to indict Miriam McCoy secretly. He wanted to serve her personally with the indictment, so he could see if she was smart enough to avoid an arrest that could land her in jail. The federal drug charges against her would cause her to be in prison for ten years to life. His goal was to quietly arrest her and convince her to work with law enforcement. He wanted everyone involved with her, including her former husband and the two girls, to help connect the Columbian cartels with her drug trade.

Mike met with the Franklin County Prosecutor Michael Miller to have the okay to indict Miriam using testimony from Peg, Ty, and himself. He and his team received the indictment, and they monitored her movements to determine a pattern of behavior.

They found she loved to play Bingo. Her favorite establishment was in Reynoldsburg, a suburb of Columbus. On a Tuesday night, Mike and *Mark Atman* parked their cruiser down the road from the Bingo Hall. With the detailed description given to him by Peg, Miriam was not hard to find. Her unnatural colored blonde hair and distinctive bust line made her stand out from the other intent game players. The two girls who worked for her were with her on the other side of her table.

Mike and his partner walked up the center aisle and crossed through the long tables to the empty spots next to and across from Miriam.

Six bingo cards lay in front of her. Mike sat by her invading her space by leaning and looking at her cards. She paused with her Bingo stamp in midair, turning to Mike and said, "Do you have a fucking problem?"

Quietly Mike replied, "No. I don't. But you might. I'm Sargent Mike Powell, and I'm with the Franklin County Drug Task Force. I have a secret indictment in my coat for your arrest. If you want to talk, you can quietly walk out with me. I don't have to place you under arrest here. But if you want to make a scene, I can slam you right here on the table. My partner and I can cuff you and cart you out of here. What do you want to do?"

She slowly put down her stamp. Leaning forward, she said, "Girls, watch my cards for me."

She turned her head to Mike and said, "Let's go outside."

Without even glancing at Mike, the girls each took three of her cards. They were concentrating so intensely on their cards; they had no idea what was happening.

After they walked outside, Mike showed Miriam the indictment. She nodded, reached in her purse for a cigarette, and while she lit it, she said, "I want to talk. I don't particularly want to go to prison."

"If you are going to talk to me, I think you'll need an attorney, and we need to seek permission to work with you."

Usually, Mike would not do this, but Miriam was too relevant to the investigation. He wanted nothing that would be questionable to happen as far as any attorney privileges.

Miriam said she had an attorney. Mike said, "Let's get your attorney on the phone right now."

Miriam, with Mike and his partner watching, took out her cell phone from her purse. She called her attorney. "*Mr. Scott*, I've got this guy here. He's law enforcement."

After hearing the attorney's name, Mike knew he was familiar with her lawyer, and the lawyer knew him. He asked Miriam to put Mike on the phone.

"I have a secret indictment for her. I don't have to serve this right now. We've talked, so I am willing to work with her. We need to talk to the prosecutor to give her credit for assisting us. If we have to take her into the system, she can't do anything with me."

Her attorney said, "Let's meet."

Mike and the attorney met that night. Mike ended up doing a 96-page summary of Miriam McCall. She verified the girls were working for her. She confirmed they were traveling to New York City, sometimes California, sometimes Florida, and sometimes Houston.

They were all connected to a Columbian man named *Carlos Wagner*, and another man, *Leonardo*. These individuals, especially Leonardo, were moving kilo amounts of cocaine through this part of the country. Leonardo worked for Wagner. Wagner worked for *Adolfo Trujillo*. Trujillo was under *Pablo Escobar*.

Miriam provided cell phone numbers that allowed law enforcement to subpoena records. Cities such as Houston, New York City, Los Angeles, and Miami were all on the list of where calls were made. Also, on the list were calls to Columbia.

As Mike continued to work with Miriam, he discovered that besides the two girls residing with her, she also involved her family in the drug conspiracy. Her former husband and their two sons owned the garage, where they had traced the dealer tags of the powder blue Corvette. Her former husband also worked to construct some of the secret compartments that carried the drugs and money.

After three months of working with Miriam, the Task Force under Mike's supervision was having her make phone calls to Leonardo and Wagner. The Task Force was fielding these phone calls when they heard this from Wagner:

"My people are still upset with the loss of eighty kilos. They think you had something to do with it. They don't know if they want to deal with you anymore. You are no longer trusted."

Once Mike heard this phone call, he contacted Miriam's attorney. Miriam understood if she lied, gave misinformation, or deceived them, her prison time would be affected. The phone call allowed them to uncover one of the major plots of her involvement before she started working with the Task Force. A plot she had neglected to mention.

It seemed Wagner had called Miriam from New York City. They had a hundred kilos of cocaine (two hundred and twenty pounds) of excess cocaine the cartel wanted to move out of the city. Wagner asked if she could find a place to store it. He also asked if she could sell some kilos while it was in the Columbus area. Miriam said she could hide it. She said they could store it at *Thomas Harris*'s apartment in Reynoldsburg. She gave Harris her complete endorsement. Wagner also liked that Harris's sister, *Annette,* and her son lived with Leonardo in Columbus. Annette also took those courier trips.

Miriam rented a vehicle, and she and her boyfriend from Cincinnati, *Bill Ables*, went to New York City to pick up a duffle bag containing the one hundred kilos. On the way back, Miriam detoured to her sister's home in Newark, Ohio, which was about forty miles from Columbus, and drop off the kilos for a few days. She wanted to make sure it was alright to take the product to Harris's location. Eventually, she was secure it was safe to take it to Harris's apartment.

She contacted another associate, *Daniel Lipo*, who would pay for quite a few of the kilos. Lipo and the other Columbians staying at Harris's place would sell twenty of the kilos, leaving eighty.

On a Sunday afternoon, Harris and his sister would leave to go across the state to a family reunion in Lima, Ohio. Miriam, knowing they were gone and knowing there were eighty kilos in the apartment, convinced Bill Ables and another friend from Cincinnati to go to the Harris's apartment disguised as policemen. A few Columbian men were staying there.

Ables and his friend knocked on the door and identified themselves as the police. The two Columbian men believed them. "The police" told the two men they had a search warrant. Ables and his friend handcuffed and put the two in an upstairs bedroom. As the two Columbians, thinking the men were real police, and they were under arrest, waited upstairs, Ables and his partner took the eighty kilos and $250,000 from the apartment.

During a few quiet hours later, it dawned on the Columbians the police were gone. The cheap handcuffs were easy to break. They ran downstairs and found the cocaine and the money were gone.

Minutes later, Miriam received a call from Wagner. He was in an extreme state of panic. Being responsible for the money, he begged Miriam to keep alert for anyone selling high-quality cocaine for a cheap price.

Harris and Annette came back from the reunion to the chaos of the situation. Both were terrified the cartel would think they had set up the robbery.

Miriam called a guy by the name of *Dusty Gerard*. She and Gerard had known each other for years. Girard bought cocaine from Miriam a few ounces at a time. She let him know she had some high-quality stuff, and she would allow one-kilo "walk" for $25,000. In Columbus, at the time, a bird or kilo was going for $35,000. Miriam arranged to meet and sell the kilo to Gerard. She also told him she had someone interested in purchasing an ounce. Gerard was pleased. He asked Miriam to let him know who the person was, and he would sell the ounce for a $1,000.

Miriam then called Wagner and told him she knew of a person selling high-quality coke for a relatively low price.

Wagner was excited. He thought he had a clue about his high-quality product. He had no reason to believe Miriam had just set up Gerard. Wagner contacted the cartel out of New York City, and through Adolfo, two Columbian hitmen were sent to Columbus. Their job was to locate the money, the lost cocaine, and kill the people responsible.

Miriam had another associate of hers, *Bill Pilton* say he had people who wanted an ounce. Pilton took Wagner and the two Columbians sent by Adolfo to Gerard's home in a van to monitor visitors.

At one point, Gerard came out of the house with his children. He walked with other adults to his car, opened the trunk, and gave the adults something. The action increased Wagner's suspicions.

Pilton called Gerard to inquire about an ounce. Gerard told him to come over to his home. When Pilton returned with coke that he bought from Gerard, Wagner field tested it. They agreed it was the purity of the lost drugs. Wagner ordered the hitmen to go in, take care of Gerard, and retrieve the drugs.

As the men screwed their silencers on their guns and placed beanies on covering their hair and ears, Wagner saw two young kids come out the back of the house. He stopped the men from continuing. "You will not kill children," he said. He then called Miriam and told her to continue to watch Gerard and see if he was the robber or had he gotten the drugs elsewhere.

Mike would confirm with Girard later that he only bought one kilo from Miriam. The rest of the kilos remain unaccounted for to present day.

Mike interviewed Miriam, and she claimed she gave some kilos back to the cartel. But there was no way she nor Mike could prove that occurred.

Once the Task Force and U.S. attorneys found out Miriam had neglected to tell them everything, instead of 8 years in jail, she ended up with 14 years of mandatory prison time.

Her two young sons received leniency since they had only sold small amounts. The acts were minor felonies. Her former husband pled guilty as to his part of the conspiracy. Both strippers, because they cooperated, did not receive any jail time. They could be on ankle bracelets as long they fulfilled the requirements of their probation. They helped to get convictions on many individuals.

Arrest of Leonardo

Shortly after the phone call from Carlos Wagner, where the Task Force stumbled onto Miriam's lies, they decided she could do more than she was doing. Mike told her to call Wagner. " See if anything is happening. Tell him you have people who have money, and if he can bring anything up, you have a buyer for one of those kilos. It doesn't matter if it's twenty-five or thirty thousand dollars."

Wagner replied, "I need to talk to my people about dealing with you again. But there may be something we can do."

Unknown to the Task Force, Leonardo had recently returned from Florida in a sleek, red Mazda 300 series. The Mazda had a secret compartment holding twenty kilograms of cocaine.

On Thanksgiving eve 1990, Miriam was making calls to reinstate herself with Adolfo and plan a drop. Miriam told Wagner. "I'll come and get the product when and wherever you want. Once I see the baggage, I'll get the money."

They agreed to do the transaction at Thomas Harris's townhouse in Reynoldsburg. Miriam called Harris to get the okay to set up the deal at his residence. The Task Force would set surveillance at Harris's apartment. At the appointed time, they saw a vehicle pull into the parking lot driven by a Columbian named *Carito España*. España carried a shoe bag with him.

The Colombians did not want Miriam to be alone in the transaction. They would drive over to the location of the buyer with the kilo and pick up the $25,000. They would return to deliver the money to España, who worked for Wagner and Leonardo. Before Marian could go into Harris's residence, they searched her and her car. They didn't want her carrying anything into the apartment.

Mariam went into the complex and came out with Harris. They drove to a phone booth at Main and McNaughton, where Miriam called Mike. She told Harris she had to check in with her connection.

As Miriam was going back to their car, two police cars came screeching to a halt and to block them. The officers arrested both Harris and Miriam. Mike identified himself to Harris after the officers had placed Miriam in a cruiser.

"Mr. Harris, I know you have a kilo of cocaine in your residence. Wherever that cocaine came from, I know there's more out there. I know your friend Leonardo is in Columbus somewhere. If you want cooperation from me, and any consideration from the courts, start talking now. I don't want you. I want the people you work for."

Harris, standing by the car with his hands cuffed, paused for a second with his head down. He sighed and then said, "Carito España is at my house. If we don't get the money back to him soon, Leonardo will know something went wrong."

Mike then ordered the SWAT team to go to Harris's townhouse and arrest España. They were to take him down to the Franklin County jail. Under no circumstances was he to make any phone calls until the team heard from Mike.

España met the leader of the SWAT team with an open mouth and wide eyes when they came quietly in through the front door using the key Harris had generously offered. The officers converged on him so quickly, España didn't have time to understand what was transpiring until he was being read his rights and cuffed. España, identified later, was one of the hitmen sent to kill Gerard.

During the interview with Harris, he identified his sister Annette as the woman living with Leonardo. Mike already knew this information. What they didn't know was where she and Leonardo were now living. It seemed Harris didn't know either. He said that he thought she would be home with Leonardo and her son. All he had to do was call her. Through the conversation, Mike found out Harris had a girlfriend who was a go-go dancer. He told Harris to call Annette and tell her he needed her help. His car had broken down, and his girlfriend needed a ride to work. He was to ask for her help.

Harris called Annette and told her the story. Annette said, "I'm on my way."

Mike ordered all cruisers and police vehicles to be moved out of sight of Harris's residence. His townhouse was in a complex, so some unmarked vehicles could stay close for backup. Mike and the two other undercover detectives made themselves at home. When Annette walked in, she thought Harris had surprised her to come to a party. When Mike pulled out his badge and identified himself to her, her response was, "Ha! Yeah, right!"

Mike's brown eyes were grave as he concentrated on her alone. "Annette, I'm very serious here. Your brother is looking at a charge of federal conspiracy, which could give him ten years to life. We got a kilo from him. You're not under arrest. I know about Leonardo. If your brother is going to get assistance when this goes to federal court, it depends on you."

As Mike said this, Annette stood in front of him, her one hand on her hip. She slowly leaned forward as if to spit in his face and said, "Fuck you! I ain't got nothing to say to you. You don't know shit about me."

Mike backed up a step and put his hands up to chest level. "Okay, fine. Then Tommy here is looking to ten to life. It's your call."

Mike asked the officers to bring Harris from the kitchen area to the front room. He stood by the officers, handcuffed. His eyes were on Annette.

Annette looked at her brother. Her face relaxed as she bit her bottom lip. She turned back to Mike and said, "Can I talk to my brother?"

Yes. Gentlemen, would you give us a moment? Kam stay."

All the officers went outside except for *Detective Kamron*. Detective Kamron was a large man. He knew his purpose was to be Mike's backup.

"Tommy, sit down against the wall, please."

Annette walked over to her brother and kneeled, putting her hand on his knee. "Honey, what do you want me to do?"

"Annette, I don't want to go to prison that long."

Annette was pale when she stood and turned to Mike. "The address is 4455 Bayshire Blvd. Leonardo is there. And so is my son. Leonardo has guns. If you guys go in there and he thinks that I'm involved, he'll kill my son."

Mike knew they had to act quickly. He sent officers downtown to make out a search warrant for the address as fast as possible. They had to get a hold of a judge that would sign that search warrant. Mike knew the U.S. Attorney and Franklin County prosecutor were on board, but they were in a rush. España had been sequestered for an hour. Leonardo hadn't heard from him for an hour. Leonardo could panic. He could leave. He could do anything.

Mike sent surveillance cars over to 4455 Bayshire Boulevard to get a description of the residence, the exact location, and to see if anyone was leaving the premises. Until they had a signed search warrant, officers were to sit on the location.

Mike asked Annette to call Leonardo to let him know she was held up. She asked if he wanted her to bring a pizza when she came home.

Leonardo thought it was a good idea. What Mike and his team didn't know was Leonardo was not upset or worried. He was watching porn films, and he had no idea how long Annette had been gone. Annette checked in several times with Leonardo, letting him know what was keeping her. Most were about her brother's car, or his girlfriend. All sounded legitimate.

An hour before midnight, the Task Force had the signed search warrant. Mike gave instructions to the SWAT team to execute the order and chose explicit officers to get the small child. He kept emphasizing that Leonardo had guns.

They exploded into the residence a bit after midnight, Thanksgiving morning. Leonardo was sleeping in the television's glow. The officers who were assigned the child went straight to his bedroom. The officers confiscated two guns, $12,000 in cash, and nineteen kilos of cocaine. Mike had called Annette's mother. She met them at the address after Mike called her to tell her it was safe for her to come. She then took the boy home.

At the Franklin County Sheriff's office, Mike interviewed Leonardo, who spoke English well. Mike knew he was a runner for Wagner, so he would have valuable information about where Wagner and Adolfo were.

Mike went over the rights waiver with Leonardo, keeping in mind not to make any errors that would cause problems in court. Mike had the practice of explaining rights to individuals who were not conversant in English. Once they said they understood and wanted to waive their rights, he would let them sign the waiver if they chose. After explaining his rights, Mike was still worried about Leonardo's comprehension. Mike asked him to read the agreement back to him. Leonardo did so with no problems.

Mike's instinct told him that Leonardo trusted him. He explained to Leonardo that if he cooperated, it would give him credit in federal court. Leonardo expressed his concern that he had family in Columbia that he would put in harm's way. It was rare to do so, but Mike worked at creating defendant and police "bond."

Leonardo offered to call Lippo. Lippo could pick up $250,000 worth of kilos tonight. Mike wanted to do this because he knew Lippo was selling large amounts of cocaine in Central Ohio. He knew, but if he did, he might also affect the case they were building.

Mike talked it over with Assistant Prosecutor Kevin Rooney. They decided not to pursue this offer. It would confuse the case and put it at risk. They wanted Leonardo in the legal system and to have the chance to debrief him thoroughly before moving forward. In examining Leonardo's phone records, they found he often made calls to Cali and Medellin, Columbia, where cartels were centered. Mike knew Leonardo could lead them to Wagner, Leonardo's supervisor.

Leonardo's Cooperation

The Sheriff's department requested the courts assign Leonardo an attorney. Once the attorney spoke to Leonardo, the attorney permitted Mike to talk to him.

Leonardo confirmed Adolfo was one of the primary people involved in the drug conspiracy. Adolfo would travel from Columbia to Mexico. He never came to Ohio, but would enter the United States, first circling to New York City to Miami, Houston, and then Los Angeles. Carlos Wagner supervised Ohio trafficking and was responsible for the cocaine trafficked to New York City. Wagner had Leonardo travel throughout the nation, transporting millions and millions of dollars. In one conversation, Leonardo described one experience.

"I was in a bedroom once that measured 12 x 16 feet with money in dominations of $100 to $5 stacked to my knees. I was continuously counting money to go into the hidden compartments of vehicles. The money I hid would go to one of the source cities."

He reported the cartel bosses would have one individual whose sole job was to count and bundle money.

Eventually, Mike would determine the case should not be in the hands of local law enforcement, but federal. He met with U.S. attorneys to continue the investigation. The goal was to indict Wagner and Adolfo and anyone else involved in the conspiracy.

Leonardo described how he and others like him in other cities would go to strip and go-go joints to recruit dancers to become drivers. The requirements were they had to have a legitimate driver's license and a clean driving record. Since they had to trust these women completely, they got to know them first. The members of the cartel would become friends, not only with the girls but also their families. Once the girls were involved with the conspiracy, cartel members were assured the girls would not steal product or money because the cartel knew where their families lived, and the girls were frequently reminded. They also had instructions never to seek hidden compartments and to only place their suitcases in the back seat of the car.

The transport of cash and product was accomplished by having built-in hidden compartments placed in mostly mid-sized sedans. Cartel members would connect and befriend local garage owners to work on the vehicles, and occasionally, these owners would install the secret compartments.

When a car was ready for pickup, the girls received a call. They would pack a couple of suitcases and head to Florida, New York, or Houston as if they were going on vacation. Reservations were made only at hotels the cartel recommended. The girls, acting as if they were on vacation, were given cash for expenses since credit cards could be traced. Once they arrived at the appointed city, the girls checked in with the cartel using untraceable phone numbers. A day or two later, cartel members would pick up the vehicle. The cash emptied by a cooperating garage owner was replaced with kilos of cocaine. The girls were notified they were to travel back to central Ohio, making sure they obeyed the speed limits or did anything that would arouse the suspicions of the police. Before leaving the city, they received instructions where to drive the car and drop it off. The drop-off points were regularly changed. The women earned a few thousand dollars each trip. They didn't touch or see either the cash or drugs in any of the transactions. When arrested and interviewed later, the girls admitted they were scared to know they were transporting either a lot of money or drugs at any given time.

One of the major connections in Central Ohio was Lipo. He would meet Leonardo or another Columbian at a designated place that was changed often. He would pick up five to thirty kilos at a time. (Later, Leonardo would testify at the sentencing hearing of Lipo.) Lipo received twenty of the kilos that were stolen by Miriam. Leonardo let Mike know he knew Miriam was involved in the one hundred kilos theft though they couldn't prove it. Leonardo also let Mike know Wagner had ordered the hit on Gerard.

Mike was able to confirm every detail of the information Leonardo gave him down to the titles of the cars used in the trafficking. He even talked to the car salesmen where the members of the cartel bought the vehicles. The importance of the task force confirming every detail was to prove to the courts that Leonardo was a truthful person. He worked with the police knowing if the cartel found out, the cartel would kill his brothers, sister, and mother still in Columbia. At one point, Leonardo's family came to Columbus, Ohio to meet with him.

For his family to visit, Mike went first to the U.S. Attorney's office and federal entities to gain permission for the family to enter the country and travel to Ohio. After they arrived in Ohio, Mike met with Leonardo's brother, sister-in-law, his nephew, and his mother down on the south side of Columbus. His mother spoke no English, so Leonardo's brother interpreted for her. As she expressed her appreciation, she gave Mike a tearful hug and thanked him for taking care of her son, even though he was involved in a major drug conspiracy. She also thanked Mike for stopping him. "I wanted none of my children to be involved in drug trafficking. You can't babysit them all the time. Leonardo made choices, and now he has to pay for them."

She brought Mike a copy of a December 1993 newspaper article from the day Pablo Escobar was killed in Columbia. The newspaper had a picture of Escobar lying in the street with several law enforcement officers around him. He had been shot trying to escape the police. It was a meaningful gift for Mike.

This visit was the last time Leonardo would see his mother alive.

Mike put Leonardo in front of the grand jury here in Ohio. Even as Leonardo was in prison, Mike would stay in touch with him. He felt Leonardo was an intelligent, respectful person who had made some stupid mistakes. Mike provided him with items such as writing material to write an account of his life. He made this account into a book, giving a copy to Mike.

Leonardo entered the Witness Protection Program with the Bureau of Prisons with only the case agent and U.S. Marshalls, who transport people knowing where he was assigned. With a new name, a new background, and a new location, Leonardo could not move around or return to Columbia without permission. He could request to leave the program at any time.

As the Task Force continued the investigation, they arrested sixteen out of the twenty indicted federally. There were a few Columbians who left the country before they could be indicted, and they disappeared. The officers never located two of the runners for the cartel.

Mike's continued concern was to locate Wagner and Adolfo.

España

Leonardo confirmed España was one of those hitmen sent to Columbus to kill Gerard. Mike would sit with España and do a proper. A proper was an agreement that España would tell the government what had transpired, and he would have immunity for anything he said. The immunity would stay unless he lied, or if he changed his statements when he went to court.

España was a former Columbian police officer. Claiming Wagner sent him to find out what happened to the one hundred kilos, he never admitted he was a hitman for the cartel. He had the iciest blue eyes Mike had ever seen, so even sitting in the room with him was unnerving. If he was looking at Mike, it was as if España saw right through him.

España was not conversant in English, which meant Mike had to use an interpreter to interview him. He did not provide as much information as was expected. He knew the conspirators and was part of the operation, but the task force could only prove he was more of a runner or gofer. If he was an assassin, the officers could not find any links that would connect him to any murders.

In the summer of 1991, Mike was home mowing the lawn when his pager went off. Shutting the mower off, he glanced at the displayed phone number but didn't recognize the area code. He went inside to answer the page.

A Houston FBI agent identified himself and said, "Are you the case agent for the case concerning Adolfo?"

"I am."

"Our agency in Houston is negotiating with Adolfo—down in Mexico. We are doing an undercover sting operation. Adolfo is supposed to come out of Mexico to Houston and sell fifty kilograms of heroin. We are meeting with Adolfo tonight. We realize you won't get here in time for the arrest, but we'd like you here tomorrow morning. Is that possible? We would like you to interview him if he agrees to cooperate."

Mike's next call was to his chain of command and the U.S. Attorney's office to get permission.

The next morning, he was on a plane to Houston. The FBI case agent made it clear Mike was going down to Houston to interview Adolfo, to identify him as the person he was seeking in his indictment, and to create what is called a "removal" hearing. Mike would appear in front of a federal judge to identify Adolfo as the individual named in the indictment. The U.S. Marshalls, if the federal judge approves, would eventually transport him to Franklin County.

When Mike arrived in Houston, he first met with Houston FBI agents and then a case agent, *George Fong,* from Orange County, the Los Angeles bureau.

"We arrested Adolfo last night in the parking lot of a Mexican Restaurant. He was wearing a three-thousand-dollar suit, a white silk shirt, and white monogrammed socks. He is an extremely arrogant man."

Mike inquired when he would interview him. Agent Fong

said they were bringing him up to be interviewed, and Mike would sit in.

When Adolfo was brought into the room and asked the very first question, he took the Fifth Amendment and requested an attorney. The interview immediately came to a halt. He basically said to Mike and Agent Fong, "Fuck you. You have nothing on me. I'll be out of here before you guys can blink an eye."

That ended the conversation. He was taken back to his cell.

Mike spent the afternoon bringing Fong up to date about the case and indictment from Ohio. Fong told Mike the Ohio indictment was registered three months before the Orange County indictment. Fong had a source that was working with the federal government concerning Adolfo and how much cocaine he was moving. It was Fong who wanted to bring Adolfo to California for trial. Fong had some wiretaps they had conducted, and pictures of thousands and thousands of kilos they could show and prove Adolfo was responsible. His department felt they had a solid case.

Mike asked, "How many kilos? What kind of weight did they get?"

Fong pulled a picture out of his case file and slid it over to Mike. The photograph showed a big box truck, the shape of a Cracker Jack™ box with the interior stacked with pallets of crates. Mike asked, "What am I looking at?"

Fong pointed at the picture. "That's our first transaction with Adolfo Trujillo out of Mexico."

"How much?"

"Turn the picture over."

Mike turned the picture over and read twenty-seven hundred kilos of cocaine.

Mike looked up at Fong. He realized his jaw had dropped open. He thought in Ohio, twenty kilos of cocaine were a lot. Fong slid another picture over to Mike. It was a location that had been shown to him by Mariam when they had taken a trip to New York City to fact find. It was also the place where the FBI had served a search warrant and took out over eight hundred kilos during their investigation.

"How many kilos can you actually show in federal court?" Mike asked.

"Fifty-eight hundred kilos of cocaine."

Doing the math quickly, Mike realized the L.A. FBI had much more in extensive proof in total weight than his case in Ohio.

Mike contacted the U.S. Attorney in Columbus to let them know about Agent Fong's case. The decision was made instead of bringing Adolfo back to Columbus, the L.A. FBI should take Adolfo back to Orange County to go to trial first. Then they would decide if they wanted to prosecute him in Ohio as well. It was backup just in case L.A. didn't get a sentence of life in prison.

Agent Fong was pleased when Mike told him the U.S. Attorney's office in Columbus was going to allow Adolfo to be tried in California first.

Within the next day, a removal hearing was scheduled in Houston. The only picture Mike had was one of Adolfo, provided to him by Leonardo. It was of Adolfo sitting in a room shirtless.

When Mike went into court that morning and was sworn in, the judge had him identify who he was and his reason to be present. Mike presented the indictment from the southern district of Ohio.

Adolfo had an attorney appointed to him. After Mike's opening statement, the prosecution was finished questioning him. It was the defense attorney's chance to grill Mike.

"Have you met Adolfo?"

"No."

"Did you ever see Adolfo as a real person?"

"No."

"Do you know if Adolfo was ever in the state of Ohio?"

"Not that I am aware of."

The defense was trying to establish doubt as to Mike identifying the defendant, his client.

The judge questioned Mike, "How are you able to identify the defendant?"

Mike answered, "I have a picture of him from a reliable source, which helped me identify him as Adolfo Trujillo."

Earlier in chambers, the judge had agreed Mike could provide the picture through the prosecutor. Only he, the judge, the prosecutor, and the defense attorney would see the image.

If Adolfo was to see the snapshot, then he would know its source. The revealing quality of the snapshot was stark. The expression of Adolfo in the picture was exactly the expression Adolfo had in court. He was sitting in the same position at a table as he was at the defense table.

The judge looked at the snapshot for ten seconds, along with the prosecutor and the defense attorney. It was of Adolfo, who was sitting in the courtroom.

The judge ruled in Mike's favor. He also ordered Adolfo could be transferred to Ohio by request of the U.S. Attorney. After Mike's identification, Agent Fong came into the courtroom. He also did his identification and request for removal. Adolfo was sent to Orange County jail.

Later, Agent Fong told Mike that once Adolfo got to Los Angeles, the cartel sent an attorney. He met with Adolfo in jail. After Adolfo saw the discovery that Ohio and California had, he knew he could no longer evade prosecution and would be found guilty. All he could do was rely on the mercy of the court by accepting responsibility for what he did. Adolfo did not want to cooperate or help the government. He wanted "acceptance of responsibility" which meant he admitted to what law enforcement had claimed. He had to confess he was wrong. If he did this, the court would reduce a life sentence to thirty years. He did not want to die in the penitentiary. He hoped he could do a minimum of thirty years and, eventually, be free.

The cartel's attorney told Adolfo the cartel did not want him to plead guilty. They wanted him to go to trial. Adolfo argued with the attorney. He knew he would be found guilty and given a life sentence. The cartel supposedly wanted him to go to trial because it would allow them to see how the government got to Adolfo and how much the government knew about the cartel's business and operations. They hoped to find who the informants were and who cooperated. It was assumed then they would put out contracts on those individuals.

Adolfo argued with the attorney. He did not want to go to trial but preferred to plead guilty and do his prison time. He was advised if he did not cooperate with the cartel, they would kill his family.

Adolfo went to trial. Leonardo was subpoenaed by the California courts to testify against Adolfo. Adolfo was sentenced to thirty-six years to life. The last Mike heard; he was serving his time in federal prison.

The Hunt for Wagner

Mike had heard the name Carlos Wagner so much, he felt he knew him. In 1992, Mike met with numerous agents from the Florida Department of Law Enforcement (FDLE) who had been working on another drug trafficking faction, which included Wagner down in the Miami area. The FDLE provided Mike with a current picture of Wagner. They were aware of Leonardo and España and some other Columbians Mike had been Investigating. The case they were working in Miami was unrelated to Adolfo and the Los Angeles connection, even though Wagner was working for Adolfo. It was common for the traffickers to have several discrete entities where they could get the cocaine. It was easy to identify Wagner as one of the main drug conspirators controlling much of Ohio and Pennsylvania, and that part of the country, but they couldn't arrest him during the initial sweep.

Mike received a call from the U.S. Attorney's office that Wagner had been arrested in Houston and was about to be extradited to Columbus. Mike called the U.S. Attorney's office in Houston to find out how Wagner had been apprehended.

The cartel had kidnapped Wagner because he owed them money from stolen drugs and for drugs confiscated by law enforcement. He was responsible for all his cartel products. The cartel had discovered he had been doing some freelancing and keeping the money for himself. Members of the cartel had taken him to a Houston hotel, cuffed him to a bed. He was to be under guard while members of his family raised the money he owed.

After four days, Wagner worked the cuffs loose from the bed while one of his captures was using the bathroom. He smashed a window, gashing his arm, and jumped. He ran into the hotel lobby, yelling he had been kidnapped.

Meanwhile, as Wagner was working his handcuffs free, a Houston off-duty policeman came into the hotel lobby. He had out-of-town relatives come to visit and needed to arrange for rooms. When Wagner ran into the lobby, dangling the cuffs, bleeding and yelling, the officer grabbed him and tried to stem the bleeding while the hotel staff called an ambulance.

Wagner told the officer drug traffickers had kidnapped him and held him in a hotel room. The officer called for assistance. When the assisting officers got an ID from Wagner, they ran a background check as he was treated in the emergency room and found that Wagner was wanted in Ohio for Federal Conspiracy charges. After treatment, they placed him under arrest.

Knowing he was safer with law enforcement than on his own, Wagner did not fight the extradition back to Columbus. He knew the cartel would not forgive his debt because he was under arrest. They would force a family member to work until the debt was paid.

Wagner had an attorney appointed for him. Mike did not have a chance to interrogate him. Wagner went to federal court and pled guilty and received life imprisonment. According to the Assistant U.S. Attorney, this was the first time in history that anyone on a drug count pled guilty and received life. Wagner had decided to face life in prison than face the cartel even though he was still terrified the cartel would find him and kill him, even in jail.

PART SIX

Michael and Shawn

The Big LSD Bust

1994

Stage One

 In early 1994, Mike, now supervisor of the Drug Task Force, received a call from the New Albany Police Department. New Albany was, and still is, a growing affluent suburb northeast of Columbus, Ohio. The officer calling told him they had just arrested a high school kid for burglarizing houses in the area. Questioning why they were calling the Franklin County undercover unit, the officer said, "Well, here's the deal. This kid wants to cooperate to minimize his sentence. He claims he has lots of connections in the drug community. We need you guys to follow up. We don't have anyone here in the NAPD to work drug cases."

Shawn and his partner, Patrick, were assigned to interview the kid. They sat down with *Johnny Winters* and a New Albany police officer. Johnny looked rough. He had shoulder-length, dirty brown hair, and bangs so long they hid his gray eyes. Baggy pants edged with his underwear complimented his wanna-be gang look. A bar pierced his septum. Shawn thought this kid looked like he was still in high school. The policeman handling the burglary charge said Johnny had just graduated from New Albany High School. At the interview, Johnny seemed nervous, but friendly and respectful enough. Johnny shook hands with Shawn and his partner when he was introduced to them. After they were seated, all Shawn said to Johnny was to tell them his story. Between constant hair tossing and changing positions, he claimed he knew people who were selling marijuana, magic mushrooms, and LSD.

During this time, LSD complaints had become rare. The drugs the unit usually had to deal with were marijuana, crack cocaine, and powdered cocaine. When Shawn and Patrick returned to the office, they immediately walked down the hall to see Sargent Mike Powell, their supervisor.

Mike leaned back in his chair. "Do you believe this, kid? You know I haven't seen any LSD in years."

"This kid claims he's so well connected to other kids, even on campus. He sets up meetings. He's never present at any of the sales. It's kind of a cool thing if he's on the level. Let's do this," Shawn said.

Mike reached his hand up to rub the back of his neck and shook his head. "Geez, we haven't had any informants on OSU's campus for hallucinogens like LSD for years. Okay, set up a defendant agreement. You need to check with the prosecutor's office because you know we can't approve this kid to work off his burglary charges without their okay. I'm sure they'll say it's only a deal if he gives us the drug dealers."

As soon as Shawn got the okay call from the prosecutor's office, he went back to Mike to let him know. They had to set up the paperwork and then figure out their plans.

Typically, when the undercovers have an informant, the informant must introduce the undercover to the suspect, the drug dealer. It's up to the detective to then "cut" out the informant, to get him or her out of the picture, to identify the drug dealer. No one wanted the informant to be called to testify. But with Johnny, he was so good at connecting people; they didn't have to cut him out, he cut himself out. He would say, "Hey, I know this guy who wants to buy from ya. Sell to him."

Shawn's first job was to come up with a cover story. All the kids in the area knew Johnny had been arrested for burglarizing houses because he was locked up for a while. Because it was so widely known, they used his being in Franklin County jail as part of the cover story. Johnny named Shawn "Ziggy." Shawn hated the nickname, but agreed it was a good cover name. The cover story was Ziggy and Johnny had been cellmates. With a lot of time on their hands, they got to talking. Johnny mentioned drugs, and Ziggy said he was a dealer. So naturally, Johnny said, "I can hook you up!"

As Shawn initially worked with Johnny, the deals were mostly high school kids in the New Albany area who had just graduated with Johnny.

On a Saturday, Shawn received a call from Johnny. "I can hook you up with this guy named *Matt Kavanaugh* if you want to do the deal. He can get you a sheet of LSD."

A sheet of LSD is 100-unit doses. To be jumping right into 100-unit doses was incredible. It never happened like this before. Shawn felt if he had to, he would beg Mike to do the deal.

Calling Mike at home, he said, "Mike, hey, I just got a call from Johnny."

"Okay, so? What's the deal?"

"Well, it's a sheet of acid."

"You're kidding me. Oh my God, a sheet?"

Mike immediately called the lieutenant of the unit to okay the overtime that would be needed to complete this deal. Budget issues made it difficult to get any overtime approved. Mike and Shawn were both shocked by how quickly the lieutenant approved it.

The next day, Shawn met with Johnny and told him to proceed. Johnny called Kavanaugh and said, "I've got Ziggy on the line. He wants to do a drug deal with you for a sheet of acid. He'll meet you at the Northern Lights Shopping Center off of Cleveland Avenue."

Johnny listened to when Kavanaugh wanted to meet. Then he told him he'd check with Ziggy about the agreed time and date.

Shawn took Patrick with him. Since Johnny had given Kavanaugh the description of Shawn's car and confirmed when they would meet, he was confident there wouldn't be any issues. Plus, if Kavanaugh said anything, he would tell him he didn't know what he was walking into, so he brought some help.

A dark blue Chevy sedan pulled up to the back of Shawn's car, but the driver didn't put it in park. He just let it idle. Shawn could see from an angle the window slowly coming down. Shawn told Patrick to wait and got out. Patrick braced to get out of the car and ready if Shawn found himself in trouble. Shawn moved slowly but purposefully with his hands in full view to the rear of his car. He made sure he didn't move to block Patrick's view of the driver.

"Hey, I'm Ziggy."

"I'm Matt."

Confused, Shawn had to ask, "Are we goin' someplace, or do you want to park and exchange here?"

"I got to go down the road and get it. I need to see your money," said Kavanaugh.

"I've got my buddy with me. You know," Shawn shrugged. His hand went slowly to his jacket pocket but was ready to dive between the cars if he had to. He brought out money to show him.

"Now, I'm not going to just give this to you. Jump in the back of my car, and I'll drive you to where you want to go."

"Man, I don't know if the guy's gonna like that."

"Ah, come on."

As an undercover, Shawn didn't want to give him the money. He wanted to know where he was getting the drugs. As it was, this was a good deal. They were paying $200 for a sheet of LSD, that's $2.00 a unit dose. Kavanaugh could have easily gotten $7.00 a dose. The price allowed Shawn, Patrick, and Mike to know the people they were about to meet were not the real drug dealers.

Kavanaugh jumped in the back of the car, and Shawn and Patrick drove him down the road to an address on Cleveland Avenue. The house was a brick double. They pulled into the back, where a couple of cars were already parked.

"Give me your money; I'll be right back," Kavanaugh said.

"No, I think I'll go in with you," Shawn said.

"Dude, my guy ain't gonna like that. He's not gonna like people in his house. He doesn't know who you are."

"Ah, come on. You'll be all right."

He agreed. The three of them went to the back door and knocked.

A clean-cut twenty-something answered the back door. He paused with the door in a half swing when he saw three men. Recognizing Kavanaugh, he turned and only said, "Come in, guys. I'm *Steve*."

Shawn and Patrick entered a place that looked like two twenty-something slobs lived there. It was a total mess. An old pizza box lay on a coffee table among laptops, beer cans, and drug paraphernalia. A blue haze of marijuana clouded the room. A four to five-feet water bong sat next to an overstuffed chair like it was a reading lamp. Shawn had never seen a water bong that large in his life.

After Shawn precisely told that to Steve, Steve seemed to take an immediate liking to Patrick and him. Steve said to Kavanaugh, "So, where's the money?"

Shawn gave the money to Kavanaugh, and then Kavanaugh gave the money to Steve. Steve wouldn't deal directly with customers. So not to take a more significant risk, the money needed to go through Kavanaugh.

"Okay, you two have a seat. We'll be right back." Steve and Kavanaugh then went upstairs. Shawn and Patrick sat down to watch Steve's roommate play a video game. Shawn said later; he didn't know if the roommate even knew Patrick talked to him. He was that crazy high.

Kavanaugh and Steve came down the stairs, and Shawn and Patrick stood to leave. They thanked Steve. Following Kavanaugh out the back door, Shawn motioned to Patrick to drive. Shawn kept a close eye on Kavanaugh to see what he was going to do. Kavanaugh opened the back door on the driver's side, so Shawn walked to the passenger side of the car and opened the back door. Patrick didn't get into the driver's side until Kavanaugh and Shawn were settled and buckled in. Patrick made it look like he was trying to stretch his legs after sitting in the house. What he was actually doing was making sure Kavanaugh would not run with the LSD.

After they were on the road, Kavanaugh gave Shawn the LSD. Shawn was glad to see Steve had securely wrapped the blotter in aluminum foil. Shawn knew, as an undercover, he didn't want to handle the LSD with his hands. LSD is absorbed through the skin. Since sunlight can also break down the drug and make it less potent, it was doubly essential to have it tightly contained.

Kavanaugh probably made twenty-five dollars off the transaction.

Shawn collected Kavanaugh's phone number, which now eliminated Johnny as the informant.

Patrick and Shawn met up with their backups and Mike Powell after they got the LSD. Shawn was proud and downright giddy. No one in area law enforcement was buying acid. Mike unfolded the foil, and he couldn't believe it either. During the early to mid-90s, it was hard to break into sources for hallucinogens. The drug unit knew the drugs were there, but it was hard to find an informant. This exchange was the first acid the whole Franklin County undercover unit had bought in years.

The blotter that Shawn and Patrick brought back was unusual. It was perforated. Shawn, Patrick, and Mike discussed how this wasn't a professional deal. Kavanaugh selling one hundred hits right away to a guy they didn't know was shocking. In the past, the team usually saw 5 to 10 strips of LSD in a first transaction. Since an undercover might have five hundred sources in a career, a detective might have 5 that could turn into something important. They agreed there seemed to be more to this than they saw at this point. It was decided they were going to spend more time on this case than they generally would. A sheet was considered a felony of the second degree.

Stage Two

Shawn and Patrick continued to buy sheets off Steve, but soon they splintered off. Kavanaugh would call and say, "Steve is out. I have this other guy. Do you want to go to him?"

Of course, they did. As undercovers, they wanted to get as many of the people involved as possible in these serious charges. The hope would be they could eventually "flip them." They were always trying to get to the next level of the drug supplier.

Most of the dealers Shawn and Patrick were buying from were eighteen or nineteen-years old. Kavanaugh and the others all wanted to be Shawn's friend. Shawn continued to sell Shawn's (Ziggy's) backstory that he had spent the last 10 years in and out of jail. In their eyes, twenty-seven-year-old "Ziggy" was badass. Many times, Kavanaugh invited "Ziggy" to play video games and hang out and drink beer with him. He once asked "Ziggy" to a high school pregame party for a football game at New Albany. "Ziggy" went and hung out with sixteen and seventeen-year-olds at a pizza joint after the football game.

Kavanaugh soon called Shawn to let him know he had a new contact that could hook Shawn up. Shawn, by himself this time, picked up Kavanaugh and a new kid, *Ozzie*. Ozzie was a skinny dude with long, stringy hair. His look included baggy pants, oversized shirts, and multiple tattoos. Shawn found out he was called Ozzie because he had "Ozzie-"tattooed on the middle knuckle of both hands. He was a big Black Sabbath fan.

Ozzie took Shawn to meet *Johnny DeMarco*. DeMarco worked at a Jiffy Lube™ while he was attending The Ohio State University. DeMarco was cleaner cut than the kids Shawn had encountered on this case. He was an average skinny, dark-haired, with brown eyes college kid. His only distinguishing characteristic was he was trying to grow a beard, which resulted in only a scruffy-looking chin. At the first meeting, Shawn needed to ask DeMarco for his phone number on the sly. Once he did that, he could cut both Ozzy and Kavanaugh out of any deals. Doing this, it would cost less money to buy the LSD since both Ozzy and Kavanaugh were making money from any buys Shawn would make with DeMarco. Shawn also knew he had enough evidence to charge Ozzy and Kavanaugh, and now he had to work on DeMarco to catch him in the net of charges. In the parking lot of the Jiffy Lube™, Shawn could meet his goal by getting DeMarco's phone number and buying a sheet of LSD.

Shawn called DeMarco soon after the first meeting. He was told to meet DeMarco at his apartment on Indianola and Ninth, right by Ohio State's campus. Shawn went without his partner to this meeting. DeMarco and his girlfriend lived in a downstairs apartment. When Shawn arrived, DeMarco looked like he was ready to leave.

"Where you going?"

"Ziggy, I don't keep a supply here. Give me the money, and I'll get the stuff."

"Right. I'm gonna wait here. Why don't I drive you and then drop you off back here?"

"No. You wait here with my girlfriend."

"Come on. You're gonna rip me off."

DeMarco pointed to the sofa. "No, I'm not. Have a seat. You're in my house with my girlfriend. I'm not gonna rip you off."

Shawn sat on the couch, and DeMarco handed him the remote to the television. Since Shawn was by himself, he was wearing a wire. Mike, supervising Shawn's backup, knew that Shawn may not convince DeMarco that he should go with him to meet his supplier. It was the team's job to find out where DeMarco was going, and to cover Shawn when DeMarco returned. Patrick, in an undercover car, followed DeMarco to OSU's Twin Towers, student housing on campus, but lost him in the traffic around the university. DeMarco returned to his apartment and completed the transaction.

Stage Three

A few weeks later, Shawn was back at DeMarco's apartment. He again tried to go along but was unsuccessful. This time, Shawn didn't want to stay with DeMarco's girlfriend. "Look, you didn't rip me off last time. Call me when you come back here."

Mike had given Shawn instructions to leave the area. He didn't want Shawn's vehicle anywhere to be spotted. Four cars were set up to follow DeMarco.

The undercover team followed DeMarco to the OSU Towers. One officer got out and followed DeMarco on foot as he went inside. The officer that stayed with DeMarco's car saw he and another guy coming toward DeMarco's car. They must have come out another door. Radioing his partner, the officer who followed DeMarco sprinted back to the surveillance car in time to follow them as they traveled to another area just off campus, Chittendon and High Street. DeMarco pulled to the curb in front of an apartment building with a single-entry door but four separate apartments. The new guy climbed out of the car and went to the entry door. No key was necessary. The undercover crew could not make out which apartment he entered.

Fifteen to twenty minutes later, a third man came out of the apartment building. They surmised he was going to pick up the LSD. The undercover crew left one car at the Chittendon address, and the last two followed this new guy. He took them up to 20th and Summit Street, now in the area of the fraternity houses of OSU's campus and parked at a strip mall with a carry-out and a laundry. He parked his car at the carry-out and walked to the north of the campus area.

One of the undercover team followed him in between two buildings and lost him. The two buildings where the unknown male could have gone were residential. One was an older apartment building with cement steps. The railing up the stairs looked newly replaced above the old lattice bordering below the front porches still had old wooden railings. The top of building had the word Cadillac in lighter brick giving the impression it was a special place in its day. The building looked well-maintained except for the wooden porch railing. Each apartment had new windows and glass block basement windows, and they all had back doors. On the other side was a single three-story house. It was also well maintained. These residences could be rentals for OSU students.

No one knew if this guy had the money for the LSD or not. The detectives returned to where the unknown man had left his car at the carry-out.

Not long after, the man they followed returned to his car. He reversed his path and returned to Chittendon, parked his car, went back into the apartment. DeMarco had been waiting in his car, not once going into the apartment building. Once the man they followed returned to the apartment building, DeMarco's companion came back out. DeMarco returned his partner to the Towers on campus and then he called Shawn to meet him at his apartment. Shawn, of course, met him and picked up the LSD.

The price for the LSD had gone up. Instead of the accepted two hundred dollars, DeMarco asked for fifty dollars more. He just shrugged when Shawn asked him why. Shawn gave him the extra fifty dollars.

When Shawn returned to make his report, they noticed the sheet looked more professionally done. The sheet was perforated, but on the first buy, it looked like someone had used an ink pen and a ruler to make the grid pattern. This grid looked like a sewing perforation which marked a perfect ½-inch x ½-inch square.

Mike, Shawn, and the team waited a week. Shawn called DeMarco directly with a request for three sheets. By this time, Ozzy and Kavanaugh were not happy with "Ziggy." They realized he had cut them out.

Stage Four

Mike Powell and the team needed to know what they had and where they stood. They needed to identify the guy in the Towers, and what apartment he went into on Chittendon. To do that, they had to contact the OSU police department to find out the name of the young man who lived in the Towers. They also needed to discover where the next guy who carried the money went to pick up the LSD at 20th and Summit.

Mike and Shawn agreed that the people they had involved in the situation were low on the chain, so they decided the team had to increase the amount of purchase of LSD so Shawn could move up the chain of command. The next contact was to ask for three-hundred-unit doses. DeMarco's reaction to Shawn's call for three sheets was, "Let me make a phone call."

He returned the call and informed Shawn that "the guy" had it. They agreed on a price. The individual price stayed at two hundred fifty dollars, taking this endeavor to seven hundred fifty dollars. The answer DeMarco gave Shawn proved to the team this case had potential, and that the amount of money the team was possibly letting "walk" would be worth it.

As before, Shawn went to DeMarco's apartment. Shawn told DeMarco he was going to drink a couple of beers while he waited for his call. This allowed Shawn to remain in the area and wait for his return call.

DeMarco left to follow his usual route. He picked up the young man at The Towers and took him over to the apartment at Chittendon. A male and female left the Chittendon location and traveled to the 20th and Summit area. The female who was driving parked by the carry-out, but only the male exited the car. The male set out on foot. Instead of casually walking, he regularly turned to see who was around. He stopped and waited, again checking if there was anyone following him. The team lost him again between the same two buildings. Ten minutes later, he re-emerged from between the buildings and headed back to the car, and the two individuals drove back to Chittendon. After they went up the steps and into the apartment building, DeMarco's contact came back out and met back up with DeMarco, who had been waiting in his car.

As they were driving back to the Towers, a siren blared off behind them. They pulled over to the curb, and an OSU police officer pulled over behind them.

"What the hell?" DeMarco said, a bit rattled, since they both knew what they had in the car.

The cop moved slightly behind the driver's window as DeMarco opened the window. "May I see your IDs, please?"

"What's going on, officer?"

"I just got a complaint that two guys in a car described like yours were just on High Street and yelled obscenities at some people who were on the sidewalk."

"It wasn't us. We didn't do it."

"Let me see your IDs, please."

Both nervously pulled out their wallets and handed their IDs to the OSU police officer. The cop walked back to his car and took his time writing information on the IDs. He finished and walked back to the driver's side and handed DeMarco their IDs. "Okay, you guys know I have your names. If we hear another complaint and the car or license number matches, we'll be knocking on your doors."

With that, the cop walked back and shut the car's lights off. DeMarco carefully pulled away and drove to The Towers. As DeMarco's contact got out of the car, another member of the undercover team, sitting on the steps by The Tower, heard him say to DeMarco, "Man! We have all this acid on us, and the cop had no idea!"

After a good laugh at the officer's expense, DeMarco returned to his apartment and called Shawn. Shawn was in the area and returned to the apartment within a reasonable amount of time. As he was receiving the three sheets of LSD, DeMarco said, "Dude, there is so much LSD right now. It's flowing like water. He's got some Alice with a dynamite lower half!"

Shawn didn't know what he meant but said, "Hey, that's cool! It's flowing like water. Great! I'll be back to order up so more. We're gonna make a lot of money!"

The surveillance team had accomplished several of their goals. The OSU policeman supplied the name of the two in the car. They knew the name of DeMarco, but now they knew the student's name to be *Morgan Anderson*. Patrick, Shawn's partner, had been given the one assignment of positioning himself so he could determine the apartment Anderson entered. The name on the lease for that apartment was *Jeffrey Wilson*. The team needed this information to execute search warrants on all these locations to tie the whole conspiracy together.

They knew the name of the owner of the car that was driven from Chittendon to 20th and Summit. It was owned by *Janice Bechet*, who was the daughter of a police officer.

Stage Five

"He's got some Alice with a dynamite lower half."

Shawn told Mike and the rest of the team working on the case DeMarco's comment. They were all guessing what it meant. One idea was maybe it was new drug jargon. The sheets Shawn brought back were different. There were little designs on them. It resembled a puzzle piece.

The prevailing thought was if the supplier had so much LSD, why not ask for a book? To anyone on the team's knowledge, no one had ever bought a book before. A book would be one thousand-unit doses. Shawn called DeMarco, "You said it was flowing like water. How much would a book cost?"

DeMarco said he would ask.

When DeMarco called back, he said, "Yeah, we can get it. Come over. We need to talk."

We need to talk? DeMarco had said nothing like that to him before. This comment put everyone on edge. Mike told Shawn. "Be cautious. We'll have back up on you."

Shawn was nervous. He thought about how many times he'd gone to DeMarco's apartment, where DeMarco and his girlfriend were smoking weed. When they were, they would ask Shawn to smoke with them. He would find some reason to say no. "Look, I'm on probation. You guys know I just got out of county jail a while ago. I can't do that, man."

Or. "I can't smoke weed. I don't want to be all screwed up driving all this LSD around."

On the way to DeMarco's apartment, Shawn wondered if that hadn't triggered some thought on their part. He worried they had figured out he was undercover. When he arrived, he followed DeMarco to the kitchen. To his girlfriend, DeMarco said, "Leave the room, okay? Go into the bedroom and shut the door."

DeMarco turned the kitchen chair around and sat. He motioned to Shawn to sit where his girlfriend was sitting. "Okay, my guys are worried about ya."

Shawn remained standing. "Why the hell are they worried about me for?"

DeMarco gestured. "Well, you're moving up awful fast. You bought a sheet a couple of weeks ago. Last week you bought three sheets, now you want an entire book. They think you're moving up really quick. You gotta be a cop. Are you a cop?"

Shawn took his time. He turned a chair around and straddled it. He brought his hand up, keeping his eye on DeMarco, and scratched his eyebrow. "No, dude. I'm not a cop."

"Smoke some weed with me to prove you're not a cop."

Putting both arms on the back of the chair, poised to move if he had to, Shawn said. "Dude, I can't. Look, dude, I have nine months on the shelf. I was lucky to get out after three months. If I get popped with dirty urine, I'm done. I can't do that. I don't want to go back to the county jail for nine months."

"Dude, I'm nervous, man. I think you're a cop."

Shawn brought his hands up. "Look, dude. I'm not a cop. You know me. We're friends. The guy who hooked me up with you, call him. He'll vouch for me."

Shawn knew Kavanaugh would vouch for him. He even went to Friday night football games with him. They had spent a lot of time together.

DeMarco stood. He moved the chair around and sat, putting his hands behind his head. Leaning back, he looked up at the ceiling. Shawn sat and observed him. His back was to the door of the kitchen. He moved his hands to grasp the back of the chair and leaned forward.

After a few seconds, DeMarco looked at Shawn. "Okay, man. I'm sorry. I shouldn't have doubted you. You're not a cop.

Shawn chatted it up with DeMarco for a while and then asked him how much he wanted him to bring for the book. He wanted $1500. It was very cheap, at only $1.50 a dose. If this was a real drug deal, they could have made $6,000 to $7000 on the transaction.

Later, Shawn talked to the task force officer running the wire car. He told Shawn he thought it was getting serious in there. He had picked up the walkie talkie and was ready to say, "Get ready, we may have to go in and save Shawn. Then you turned it around. I was prepared to send the SWAT team in to rescue you, and then ten minutes later, your guy apologized."

Stage Six

Mike had to go to his superiors to allow $1500 to walk. Usually, the maximum amount would be five hundred dollars. To give the okay to go over the maximum showed Mike and Shawn how much confidence the higher-ranked individuals had in them and their team. They also had more support from the Franklin County prosecutor's office.

Shawn met DeMarco to give him the $1500 in cash. He left the area to wait for DeMarco's call that he had the book. Mike took over from there. He planned to see if the drug perpetrators continued the same pattern and to spot which building the unknown male would enter.

After Shawn left the area, DeMarco went to the Towers on OSU's campus. Now knowing the name of the college kid, they knew which Tower and room he was residing. DeMarco took Anderson to the apartment. The deputies knew which apartment he would enter and the name on the lease but didn't know the name of the person in the apartment. They knew who the owner of the car was because they had run the tag. They knew the girl who owned the car lived in Westerville, another suburb in the area, but they didn't know how much she was involved. She seemed to be only the owner/driver of the car and very low on the ladder of involvement.

Mike had set up a lot of surveillance in the area of 20th and Summit. He sent officers on foot to cover the two buildings. Mike positioned himself in the parking lot between the two buildings.

The same pattern continued until the unidentified male parked at the small carry out and walked. Mike heard on his radio what the perpetrator (the unidentified male) was wearing and where he was. Once he was near where Mike was, Mike acted like a resident in the area, looking for his dog. He called out for Rex.

As the perpetrator walked right in front of Mike, Mike called out, "Hey, you didn't happen to see this little Yorkie? His name is Rex."

"I didn't see any dog."

"I appreciate it. Rex got loose. I'm trying to find him."

The perpetrator just nodded. Mike thought he had made conversation with the guy who had the $1500. He passed Mike and went into the building to Mike's right, the three-story house. Now they had the building where he entered, and they were closer to be able to obtain search warrants for all the locations.

When the male exited the house, he left by the same door he had entered. He walked fast, but often turned to look over his shoulder or turned his whole body to make sure no one followed him. The surveillance team kept a close watch as he returned to the car by the carryout.

The routine continued until DeMarco went to his apartment and called Shawn. Shawn was listening to all the events on his walkie talkie and knew to expect DeMarco's call, but he took his time to travel to the apartment to claim the book of LSD.

When he returned to the team's office, Shawn showed the book of LSD to Mike. DeMarco had given him the book and a picture of Alice in Wonderland.

Stage Seven

An excellent printer had copied a clear picture. On the front, Alice was walking into the Looking Glass. On the back of the cover, Alice's face could be seen as she came through the Looking Glass. Now they knew when Shawn bought the three sheets, that was only a corner of the picture. During the debriefing, the team deciphered the comment DeMarco told Shawn. "It's flowing like water." The perpetrators seem to have access to a lot of liquid acid. They were coating the paper and Alice's picture by soaking the paper in liquid acid. The second part of "Dynamite lower half" was still a mystery.

DeMarco was okay with Shawn. This buy was the third time Shawn had bought LSD from him, and he saw no sign of cops.

All the time this was going down with DeMarco, Patrick and Shawn were still buying from Steve on Cleveland Avenue. They had to keep the buys within seventy-two hours, so they had a reason for a search warrant. They had to tell a judge they had purchased the drugs recently.

Mike now had to figure out the next step and how to learn who was in the house where the unidentified male entered. Through the county auditor, they discovered that parents of a deputy sheriff owned the house at 2011 Summit Street. They would lease it to OSU students. They also could find the floor plan of this remodeled structure. It had a common area and seven different rooms. There was one lease signed for the common area, and seven rentals were separate for the seven different bedrooms. The team did not know from which bedroom the unidentified male was purchasing the acid. Mike knew it wasn't from the common area because the purchase would be in front of everybody.

They wanted to prepare the search warrants for that night. The team quickly had search warrants for the Cleveland Avenue house, DeMarco's place, the room at the Towers, the apartment on Chittendon, but 2011 Summit was a problem.

Mike checked with the Prosecutor, who felt one search warrant would cover the entire house. This idea didn't sit well with Mike. He was bothered by not knowing which bedroom was the location of the LSD. They didn't have probable cause over one bedroom or another. He would prefer they had one search warrant for the common area and seven individual warrants for each bedroom. The U.S. Attorney's Office lawyer felt there was probable cause for the common area but not the bedrooms.

Mike disagreed. He wanted eight warrants, so they would go with the state search warrants, not federal. The next step was to a judge. They went to Judge Anne Taylor, who was the duty judge for anticipatory search warrants.

Judge Taylor agreed with Mike. If they found what they needed in the first bedroom, she warned, she wanted them to minimize the intrusion of the other six bedrooms. She didn't object to searching the additional bedrooms because others may be involved, but to mitigate the searches.

In total, they drew up eleven anticipatory search warrants. This meant they had to see the same pattern they had seen in the previous three buys. Once Shawn had the LSD, all the search warrants became good.

The unit set up a considerable amount of surveillance officers. They didn't have enough people in their unit, so they pulled in other detectives and SWAT members and put them in plain clothes.

Shawn contacted DeMarco to set up another book buy. Again, DeMarco said it would cost $1500. They didn't want to increase the amount, so some of the drug would remain in the residence. They also pre-recorded the money in hopes they would grab someone with it. The pattern unfolded. DeMarco to Anderson in the Towers, Anderson to Chittendon. Their unidentified guy with the girl drove to Summit.

The goal was once the guy left Summit and returned to the car and girlfriend; they would not let him leave the carryout parking lot. Mike and three others were assigned to arrest him and the girl. The search warrant people were not to do anything until it was confirmed they had the LSD.

Once the money carrier was in the car at the carryout and his door closed, a car pulled into the driveway and blocked their exit. Mike and his team approached the car. One undercover cop, standing slightly in the back of the driver's side door, asked the girl to step out of the vehicle. She opened the car door and was moved immediately away from the car. The unknown male yelled to her, "Keep your mouth shut!"

On the other side, Mike asked the male to step out. He refused. Another team member moved to back up Mike with his gun drawn. Mike asked him again to step out of the car. When he didn't, Mike opened the car door for him. It was quickly determined the male didn't have a weapon. The girl was yelling.

When Mike moved to remove the male from the car, the other cop holstered his gun and help grab the male. The guy fought and screamed. Mike finally grabbed the male by his privates, while another detective grabbed one of his legs. It took three of the detectives to carry him out of the car and wrestled him to the ground. Still fighting, Mike straddled him and locked handcuffs on him. The other detectives had to hold him down. All were winded as they carried him, still kicking into the back of a patrol car.

A fourth man searched the car and found the LSD. Once they had the girl and the male under arrest, they signaled the rest of the team, including Shawn, to execute the other search warrants.

The male's name was *Sam Glock*. He was under the influence of a substance and tripping. Janice Bechet was his girlfriend. She was driving because Glock had had his license revoked. It was determined later all Bechet got out of the deal was gas money.

Stage Eight

Shawn's job was to execute the search warrants at 2011 Summit where Glock had got the LSD. The door was unlocked. They scanned the common area. No one was there. The first room proved to be just a bedroom, clothes, and a desk with books. The second room they entered was where they found the operation. The amount of LSD confiscated was over twenty thousand doses. After the operation was debriefed, it was determined this bust was the biggest LSD haul in the recollection of anyone in the Franklin County Sheriff's Department, even currently in the State of Ohio. This amount was above the one thousand Shawn had just bought.

The next goal was to find the money" from the transaction. When the SWAT team secured the rooms, a recently flushed toilet was in one bathroom. What clued them in was a floating bill. They instantly took the commode apart and found the rest of the money in the trap. All $1500 were recovered. Glock was a significant player in this organization, but they determined another individual was involved at this location. Someone else had to flush the money.

In the other sites included in this part of the case, they found magic mushrooms, marijuana, tons of drug paraphernalia – all minor offenses. They did not confiscate large amounts of drugs.

Shawn and the squad still had to return to Cleveland Avenue for *Steve Newberry*, their first contact.

Shawn and the SWAT team first announced their presence by pounding on the door. "Steve Newberry! Open up! Franklin County Sheriff! Police!"

There was no answer to either the front or the back of the residence. The SWAT team rammed down the front door while other police covered the back door and side window. Shawn and two others swept the downstairs and basement while the SWAT team hit the stairs to the bedrooms. No one else was in the residence.

Shawn heard BLAM! BLAM! Gunshots. Newberry was shooting at the SWAT team through his bedroom door. SWAT returned fire.

"I give up! I give up! I give up!"

"Officers hit! Officer Down!"

Shawn stood at the base of the stairs waiting to see what, if anything, he could do. There wasn't enough space for anyone else in the second-floor hall.

Two of the SWAT team members came down first. Bullets had hit their ballistic helmets. Shawn heard sirens in the distance. Two others were guiding Newberry down the stairs, one in front and the other in the back. Newberry, not wounded, had his hands in handcuffs. Shawn knew they had already read him his rights. Shawn walked out to the front yard. An ambulance raced into the driveway, paramedics opened the side doors and ran to the back of the truck almost in one fluid motion. One paramedic grabbed her bag and ran by Shawn to locate the officer, who was wounded and still upstairs. The flashing blue, red, and white lights now reflected off the surrounding buildings. Neighbors were coming out of their buildings or looking out their windows.

Stage Nine

Even though the raid was successful, the team knew there was another guy out there. That guy was still the key person in disseminating high amounts of LSD. Someone had to be supplying Glock.

They returned to Kavanaugh to see if he would continue to cooperate with them. When Kavanaugh found out Shawn was a cop, he was angry. He had considered Shawn a friend and felt betrayed. After a two-week cooling-off period, he came around and said he would continue to help but needed time to get back into the good graces of some of his contacts. They were now leery of him and thought him to be a snitch.

One month later, Kavanaugh called and said he had a contact. The price of the LSD had gone up. It was now three hundred dollars a sheet. A meeting was set up for Shawn to meet *Drew Meskimen*. Meskimen was a lower-level guy. Kavanaugh told Shawn, "You need to go over to the Kroger on High Street and North Broadway to a payphone."

To avoid suspicion, this time Kavanaugh was with Shawn for this meetup. Meskimen met them at the payphone. Shawn thought Meskimen must live close or didn't trust them even to see his car. Once introductions were over, Meskimen went to the payphone and called his contact. The contact told him to come over. According to Meskimen, when Shawn asked to join him, he claimed his contact was pretty clear, no one else.

Shawn gave Meskimen the three hundred dollars. He walked across the Kroger parking lot, across N. Broadway to a neighborhood. Being cautious, he walked through alleys, doubled back, and went through side streets. The surveillance could only get a general location. Meskimen had been careful. He walked back to Kroger differently than he did initially, crossed N. Broadway and reconnected with Shawn and Kavanaugh. He climbed into Shawn's car and handed him the LSD. After not saying anything further, he exited Shawn's car and went into Kroger. The transaction was complete.

Kavanaugh and Shawn waited a full week before contacting Meskimen again. They ordered a sheet of acid. They were told to meet at the Kroger at High and N. Broadway again. This time when Meskimen called, his contact said, "I'll be ready soon. I'll call the payphone when I'm ready."

This answer surprised Shawn since they had planned to meet, plus it was nine in the evening. They waited a full hour, but the guy didn't call back. Shawn felt like a babysitter trying to keep Meskimen chatted up during the wait time. Since he had a party to attend, Meskimen was getting impatient. Meskimen called his guy again, but he still wasn't ready. Meskimen came over to the driver's side of Shawn's car and told him, "I'm not waiting."

With that, he walked to another part of the parking lot, got in a car, and drove away. Shawn tried to see his license plate, but he was too far away, and he didn't exactly want to be seen running him down to spot it.

Shawn let Mike and the surveillance team know what happened, but then told them he and Kavanaugh were going to stick around to see if the phone rang. They all agreed to call it in an hour.

Suddenly, twenty minutes later, the phone rang. Shawn and Kavanaugh looked at each other. Kavanaugh said, "Now what?"

Shawn said, "Go answer it."

Kavanaugh said, "What?"

"Go answer it."

Kavanaugh got out of the car, walked up to the phone, slowly picked up the receiver, and put the receiver up to his ear. "No, this isn't Drew. Drew had to leave, but I'm Drew's friend."

Shawn had followed Kavanaugh to the phone.

"Can you get Drew?" Shawn heard a voice say.

"No, I don't even know where Drew's at! All he said was he was going to a party."

"Do you still want this?"

"Absolutely. I want it."

"Okay, come on over."

Kavanaugh was given the pay phone number, the address, and directions. Their surveillance followed. They watched Kavanaugh take a direct route to the address and walk into a house. Kavanaugh made the drug buy, came back, and gave the sheet to Shawn. Kavanaugh was pale, and a bit shaken. After leaving the Kroger parking lot, Kavanaugh said, "Damn!"

Shawn looked at him and said, "Hey, dude. You did good."

"That was fucking weird."

"What?"

"Walking in and knowing you guys were following me. But it was cool."

Shawn laughed.

The team no longer had to use Meskimen. The plan was to wait a week, order another buy, and use Kavanaugh for the pickup. They had an anticipatory search warrant signed by a judge ready to execute.

Kavanaugh called in. The key person said, "I have your sheet. Come on over and get it."

With this short answer, the search warrant became legal.

Stage Ten

The SWAT team entered using flashbangs and knee knockers. The wood objects fired out of weapons bounced around the rooms. They got attention and knocked down anyone who was in the area.

SWAT found *Adam Strapinski* in the bedroom. One of the knee knockers had come through the window and hit Strapinski square in the face and broke his nose. They arrested him and called an ambulance.

The team started the search but weren't finding very much. One searcher picked up what looked like a television manual. As he opened the manual, a piece of purple construction paper fell out. Also in the room was a pad of construction paper with missing sheets. Other members of the team found an aluminum paint pan, an empty spray bottle, and some fishing line.

Later, Mike interviewed Strapinski. He said, "We found the acid in the manual. You're looking at some serious time. A felony one, at least."

Strapinski countered, looking at Mike. "That's a one-unit dose."

The piece of construction paper was 6 ½ by 9 ½ inches. Mike responded, "Yeah. That's a one-unit dose for the Jolly Green Giant."

Strapinski smirked, not appreciating Mike's humor. After they arrested Strapinski, they seized several thousand-unit doses of liquid LSD from his house.

Strapinski hired a very high-priced Central Ohio defense attorney. In an interview which included Mike and Shawn, Strapinski, and his attorney, Strapinski started to lie to the officers about what they found. The attorney turned to Strapinski. "Quite bullshitting these officers and tell them the truth. If you don't, I'm not going to have you as my client."

Strapinski confessed he was Glock's supplier. He also identified his supplier of the liquid LSD in Columbus. This connection only lived a few blocks from him on N. Broadway. Mike and Shawn then suggested Strapinski give them the name of this contact so the lawyer could ask for a lower charge or less time served. With the advice of his attorney, Stravinsky said he would work with the undercover unit and gave them the name of *Joe Larson*.

The team figured out Strapinski was laying the blotter paper into the aluminum paint pan. He would then saturate the paper with liquid LSD. If there was any runoff, it would stay in the aluminum pan; therefore, he would not lose any of the LSD. After saturating the paper, he would use the fishing line to hang the paper with the liquid LSD. The higher concentration of LSD would gravitate to the lower part of the paper. That's what DeMarco meant when he said, "the dynamite lower half." He and his crew were selling thousands of hits of LSD throughout the campus area. All these individuals they were following for months were intertwined.

Stage Eleven

Strapinski identified the next guy up the ladder in Columbus. That individual, *Joe Larson*, only lived a few blocks from him on North Broadway. Strapinski, using information to lower his charges, told Mike and Shawn that Larson got the liquid LSD from Cleveland, Ohio. The contact in Cleveland received the LSD from Santa Cruz, California.

According to the agreement he made with Mike's team, Strapinski tried to get Larson to deal, but Larson said no. He was certain Strapinski was working for the cops. "I want nothing to do with you." He said as the cops listened in.

Even with this situation, Patrick and Shawn did a lot of phone analysis. After they got Larson's phone number from Strapinski, they subpoenaed Larson's phone records. They determined the phone number in Cleveland that Larson called regularly. From the phone tolls in Cleveland, they could get the number the Cleveland prospects were calling in Santa Cruz.

Strapinski's information agreed with the records they uncovered.

Shawn called Cleveland's DEA to tell them what they had. Cleveland's DEA Officer *Bryan Kennedy* said they would work it on their end. Shawn also called the Santa Cruz Narcotics Bureau. He talked to a Santa Cruz Detective *Carmen Paulsen* and told her the whole story. Paulsen called back to tell Shawn they were working on the lab information.

Shawn received a call a couple of weeks later from both police departments. Kennedy said they had an address they believed to be connected. They were doing surveillance on the address and thought they had good intel. They identified Cleveland people who were connected to the case.

Paulsen in Santa Cruz related "It is interesting what we have here. The phone number you supplied came back to a hippy compound on a hill or mountain logging hill."

Shawn said, "That's got to be it!"

Paulsen said, "We found it impossible to do surveillance on the compound since it was gated, but we did a series of flyovers. It definitely looks like a hippy compound. One of the interesting things is we subpoenaed some records on this place. We wanted to know who was leasing the property. The party that is leasing this property is also leasing a record producing company in San Francisco. This record producing company has produced one of the Grateful Dead albums."

Patrick and Shawn had continued to work on other cases. Returning after a grueling three-day trip following up on a stolen property ring in Kentucky, Shawn's phone rang at 10 p.m. It was Cleveland DEA.

In a previous conversation with Strapinski, he had told Shawn about a "hippy" looking van with California tags that brought in supplies. Shawn related this to the Cleveland DEA.

"Shawn, the hippy van is at the address we've been watching. We have eyes on it now."

Patrick and Shawn wanted to report to Cleveland immediately. The supervisor above Mike refused their request to go to Cleveland because they had been on the stolen property case for three days.

Shawn called Detective Kennedy and told him their supervisor refused permission for them to travel. "Please let us know what's going on so I can call my contact in Santa Cruz."

Cleveland officials saw the van leave the house and followed it. But they didn't keep surveillance on the residence. After they stopped and advanced on the van, one officer heard the driver yell into his cell. "We're being stopped by the cops. Get everything out of that house!"

A search of the vehicle found it empty. The team had followed the van when it was leaving. They had just dropped off the cargo. The team scurried back to the house. By the time they convinced a judge to sign a search warrant and enter the house, the occupants had left. The lights were out, and it was clean as if no one was ever there.

Shawn was furious. The case had fallen apart. He called Paulsen. Since it was Saturday, the detective was not available until Monday.

Monday, the Santa Cruz police went after a search warrant for the compound. They executed the search warrant.

"Shawn, I hate to tell you this. Everybody's gone."

The Cleveland and Santa Cruz connections had evaporated.

PART SEVEN

A New Challenge

Mike

In 1995, Mike was asked to supervise the Columbus FBI-Drug
Task Force. The goal was to dismantle drug trafficking
organizations that were affecting the United States, not just
Central Ohio. In between June 1995 and January 2002, the
Task Force conducted long-term cases that included
hundreds of hours of surveillance on known targets
associated with drug trafficking organizations, wiretaps, and
interviews/interrogations. They traveled to New York City to
meet with New York FBI agents to investigate cocaine
trafficking from New York to the Columbus and Dayton
areas.

In the summer of 1998, Mike was nominated by the
Sheriff's Office to attend the FBI National Academy. Few
officers have this opportunity, and it was one more highlight
of his career. He attended starting in January 1999 and
graduated with the 196th Academy Class in March 1999. The
Academy gave supervisors and administrators of law
enforcement entities advanced schooling in supervising and
leadership. Taking courses in management, professional
conduct, ethics courses, Mike also took classes in current drug
trends and interrogation techniques.

Mike decided in the summer of 2001 that he wanted to
transfer from the FBI back to the Franklin County Sheriff's
office so he could complete his career locally. His transfer was
granted. He was to move back on September 17, 2001. After the
9/11 attacks, the FBI requested he stay to help run leads or tips
from the public that might lead to terrorism in Central Ohio.
None of the leads he processed led to any instances.

Finally in January 2002, Mike transferred back to the Sheriff
Department and was assigned to supervise street-level drug
investigations. In the spring of that year, Deputies Steve

Tucker and Joe Vince came to the undercover unit and suggested creating a new program. They were in the D.A.R.E unit (Drug Abuse Resistance Education) for the Sheriff's Office. The purpose of the D.A.R. E. program was to teach students to make the right decisions across all levels of education. Tucker and Vince were convinced that the students knew more about drugs than the school resource officers, teachers, administrators, and parents. They thought a more significant impact could be made if all entities connected to drug abuse could be reached. Tucker and Vince wanted to combine the knowledge that Mike had from working in the undercover field to create a relevant and timely program to reach schools, businesses, and people at home.

Mike sat down with Tucker and Vince and Detective Dave Hunt and brainstormed the idea. Hunt wrote the program, and Tucker came up with the name Operation: Street Smart. Tucker wrote the grant that made it all possible. In May 2002, they began lecturing.

Shawn

Shawn became a Sergeant in 1999. This elevated him to supervisor status that included a new role of responsibility. In 2004, he was selected to attend the FBI National Academy in Quantico, Virginia. He struggled to believe that a kid who barely made it out of high school and never went to college could be selected for such an honor.

That same year, he was promoted to unit commander (lieutenant) in charge of the undercover unit. The honors continued. He was selected to attend the Drug Enforcement Administration (DEA) Unit Commanders Academy, which took him back to Quantico.

Shawn had just returned from Quantico when he received a call that startled him out of sound sleep. "Lieutenant, this is Sergeant Barrick. We lost Marty."

It had taken Shawn a bit to find his cell; he was disoriented. "What do you mean we lost, Marty?"

"Marty was in an accident, and we lost him." Barrick whispered, trying to control his emotion. Shawn, knowing Barrick, knew he was tearing up.

Shawn sat for a minute, rubbed his face, and reality took hold. He felt a chill. "Where you at?"

Getting the location from Barrick, he was dressed in ten minutes. He checked for his keys and ID as he headed out the door and to the accident scene.

Shawn saw the lights from medics, firetrucks, and police cruisers as he made his way down the highway's berm. The freeway was shut down. The highway patrol was rerouting traffic. Shawn had to show his ID initially to make his way this far. He parked his vehicle in the divider to avoid impeding emergency vehicles. The officer's car was still on its side.

Shawn braced himself to hold on to his emotions as he

walked up to the scene. Finding the Officer in Charge, he asked," What happened?"

"The heavy rain caused puddling on the freeway," the officer shrugged. "The driver lost control, and the vehicle went into the median and rolled over, killing Officer Martin."

"How's his partner?" Shawn had to pause. He was fighting back tears.

"The paramedics said he was serious." He cleared his throat. "I was getting ready to leave and head to Marty's house to let his wife know Marty was gone."

"I'm his supervisor. I'll go with you."

Marty's home was on several acres away from the city. Because of the cloud cover, they had to turn on their flashlights to make it to the walkway of the two-story house. The two uniforms went to the front door and stood on the stoop. Shawn stayed on the walk. He stared at the glowing white of the front door. The uniforms knocked once. Twice. Waited a bit. Three times. As they waited, a slowly creeping fog seemed to add to the sorrowful circumstances. Through the small glass window positioned at the top of the door, he saw an upstairs hall light go on. All their heads went down when the porch light came on. Marty's wife, Jodi, opened the door.

She paused and stood there. Her eyes first resting on the two uniformed men. She was pale to begin with, but the lighting and comprehension turned her skin ashen. When her eyes acknowledged Shawn, they widened, and tears welled up. The sound that came from her was guttural from her depths. The two officers gave Shawn room as he stepped forward and led her inside to sit down.

Jodi's body was thin from her own fight with terminal cancer. Shawn felt her shaking. "Shawn, this was supposed to be me who dies, not Marty."

One of the other officers found tissues and brought the box to her. Jodi took one and told him, "This was supposed to be me who dies, not Marty."

Shawn couldn't hold back his own tears. "Jody, you know what we thought of Marty. He was an awesome detective and officer. What can we do to help you?"

Jodi shook her head. "This was supposed to be me who dies, not Marty."

Shawn had been teaching classes on Methamphetamine Labs and other drug issues to groups. Mike knew of his reputation as an excellent speaker, so when Dave Hunt wanted to be reassigned to another unit and would no longer be working with Operation: Street Smart, he asked Shawn to join the team. Shawn knew a few things about Operation: Street Smart. He knew it was an adult drug prevention program in the community, and it was well-received. Shawn jumped at the chance to work and lecture with Mike.

PART EIGHT

Mike and Shawn

High-Intensity Drug Trafficking Area (HIDTA)

Operation Street Smart Ohio

Global Drug Concepts

In 2018, after training several deputies on how to conduct the lectures, Shawn and Mike left the Sheriff's office. In January 2019, they worked directly with the High-Intensity Drug Trafficking Area (HIDTA). They would do the same type of program but re-name it, Street Smart Ohio. They wanted to make sure they did not conflict with the Sheriff's Office Operation: Street Smart in Franklin County.

While working undercover, Mike and Shawn thought they knew about drugs and drug abuse. In speaking to the public and different institutions in the drug counseling area, they became cognizant of the number of individuals whose lives have been destroyed by this disease. As they talked to community members, Mike and Shawn realized how important it was for family members and loved ones to know the signs of early drug use and how to intervene to help an individual versus enabling him or her. Through their own education and training, they found there was a difference between dependency and addiction. As they continued to lecture, although organizers of groups brought large numbers to hear them, they were disappointed to learn that many families would not come to training until a problem occurred.

After their lectures, people would stop them and ask them to give advice about intervention. This caused Mike to research and train to conduct them. Together, Mike and Shawn launched their own business (Global Drug Concepts) and become certified by the Ohio Chemical Dependency Board. This would allow both to become Prevention Specialist Assistants. Fifty credit hours later, they felt they had a well-rounded view of substance use extending from experimentation to dependency to addiction. Because of this new training, they realized how little they knew previously about substance abuse disorder.

When Shawn and Mike lectured throughout the United States, mothers, fathers, siblings, and best friends of individuals who struggled with the substance abuse disorder approach them and asked about specific drugs or items used to ingest or hide the substances. They asked where they could go for help, so Mike and Shawn researched the many facilities of out-patient, intensive out-patient, and aftercare programs, and they shared that information. Many times, they would be asked, "Why didn't I know this information so long when the use/abuse first started?"

Mike and Shawn added the early indicators of use to all their sessions and what to do if they were seen.

The stories they have heard after sessions were heart rendering.

***

Mike was lecturing at a local high school in suburban Columbus on a Saturday for three hours to over seventy attendees. After the session, a mother came up to him and asked if she could speak to him privately. He said yes and took her to the backstage of where he was speaking. "Mike, I lost my nineteen...," breaking down in tears, she stopped. "You said in your lecture that some people use small pieces of sandpaper to shave their drugs, you know pills, down so they can then snort the drug."

"Yes," Mike agreed. "We hear that many times about sandpaper."

She nodded still fighting for control. "My daughter's father and I lost our daughter two years ago. We saw changes in her behavior. She lost interest in doing things here at school and at home. These were things she loved to do. Her grades dropped. She was very withdrawn from our family and just stayed in her bedroom for long periods of time. She didn't hang around the same friends she had since elementary school. The mom cleared her throat. "Her new friends didn't come into our house like her old friends. They would just beep the horn, and she'd go out and leave with them."

Mike could only listen as she struggled with her emotions.

"She stole and lied not only to us but to her grandparents, who she loved so very much. Her dad and I (we weren't married) thought she might be using some type of drug then, so we constantly searched her belongings and her room. I don't know how many times I searched her room while she was at school. But I found nothing."

"One morning, I was really missing her after she died, so I went out and bought her favorite color of paint. I searched her room one more time and didn't find any type of drug. So, I moved the furniture and started to paint the walls. I only worked for a minute or two when..." Again, she sobbed. "I'm so sorry."

Mike replied, "It's okay. I understand."

She started again, taking a deep breath, " I searched for drugs, but I didn't find any, but I found a small piece of sandpaper beside her bed in her nightstand. I picked it up, but since it meant nothing to me, I threw it in the trash. Had I known two years ago what you taught me today about the sandpaper, my daughter would still be alive."

Mike felt horrible that she didn't know. Maybe her daughter would be alive and perhaps not, but at least if the mother had known, she would have had a chance to help her.

***

In September 2017, Mike was lecturing at another high school in the Columbus area for two health teachers that he had known for almost ten years. They would ask him to come into their health classes each semester, and he would teach each of their class periods and talk about substance use and abuse. Most of the kids would tell him they knew someone they cared about abusing a drug. Mike never asked for names, but he would share some indicators that would alert them to the use of harder drugs. He talked to them about needles and cooker type items such as spoons. He warned them of certain items such as metal or stainless-steel hose clamps with slots that were used to shave pills down for snorting. In April 2018, Mike was setting up to do a session for the teachers' second-semester classes, when a young man came up to him, put his arms around him and hugged him.

"Well, thanks, young man! What's your name?"

The young man told him and then said, "You saved my uncle's life!"

Mike stepped back after seeing the boy's eyes were teary. "What do you mean?"

"I was in last semester's health class when you talked about those hose clamps. During Christmas break, my family went to my uncle's house. My uncle has lots of video games, so I went into his room to play some, and I saw an open metal hose clamp on the nightstand. I knew right away what my uncle was doing. My family knew that my uncle was struggling with issues and suspected he was using drugs, but nobody was sure."

The boy shrugged. "I told my dad. He confronted my uncle."

Mike nodded. "Good for you. What happened next?"

"My uncle admitted he was shaving pills down and snorting them."

Mike looked at the health teacher, who was as surprised and moved as Mike. "My dad persuaded him to get help, and he's in recovery."

Mike smiled and said, "That's good news. How about another hug?"

***

After one session, Shawn and Mike were approached by a mother and father. They wanted to share how they found out their teenage son was using some dangerous prescription drugs. "He was showing signs they suspected could be related to drug use. We searched his car, his belongings, and his room for drugs, but we seldom found anything other than maybe a pipe for weed and eye drops."

The father went on, "We felt he was only doing some marijuana and alcohol. Then one day, our son wasn't home, and I was searching his bedroom. I noticed a screw on the floor and looked up to see it was from the air vent. I was getting ready to reach up and put the screw back in the vent when I noticed some fine white powder on the threads. It couldn't be drywall, so I took it to be tested. It came back Percocet (oxycodone)."

Shawn asked, "What did you do?"

The father shrugged. "We confronted him, and he agreed to go into treatment."

"How is he now?"

"He is doing well and back in school."

***

In a session with a Heating and Cooling company, four men asked Shawn and Mike to sit down with them. They were feeling guilty for not helping a colleague who they all liked.

MJ had come up from West Virginia. After going through a nasty divorce, he wanted a chance to start over. He had found Christianity and didn't drink or smoke. MJ was assigned to their team, and they set about showing him the ropes.

They loved how fast he learned how to set things up and take care of customers. He was funny, and they really enjoyed working with him. He was into his family that consisted only of his mom and daughter.

One week, he told them how he was putting his daughter's room together because she was coming for a visit. He bought new things at Target and went on about sheets, a light, and even a dresser. He was going down to get her Friday night, and they were going to spend the weekend together. The guys told him about some places he could take her that wouldn't cost a lot.

The Monday after the daughter was supposed to visit, MJ wasn't himself. He was down. It turns out he got to his ex-wife's place, and she refused to let him see his daughter leastwise let her spend the weekend with him. He worried about the cost of rehiring an attorney and taking her to court again.

After that, MJ was different. He was working hard still, but he was not the same MJ. Next, he started being a bit late for work, and the team would get a late start on calls. The guys covered for him. They felt he was going through a rough patch.

Soon after, they found out MJ was going out to bars and strip joints. He wanted to hook up with girls and have a good time.

They spent a couple of weeks covering for him until one day he didn't show up for work at all. One guy called his cell. MJ didn't answer. Another guy called his mom in West Virginia to see if she had heard from him or if he had gone down to visit. She hadn't heard from him. She said she was worried and would be up to Columbus in a few hours.

In the afternoon, the guy who had called his mom heard from her. She asked if they had heard from MJ. They said no. "I'm at his apartment, but he's not answering the door. I'm going to call the police because I can't reach his landlord."

The police came. Finally, the landlord was reached, and his mom and the police found MJ. He was lying in his bed, dead from an overdose. The men he worked with felt terrible. They realized they should have told someone, their supervisor, anyone who might have helped.

***

A mother told Mike of her daughter's story.

My daughter, *Tracey*, started smoking weed and drinking in high school. Eventually, she was doing pills and cocaine, and almost anything she could get her hands on. After overdosing and nearly dying, she agreed to go to in-patient treatment for ninety days. She completed the in-patient treatment and was committed to staying sober. She was in her mid-twenties.

She finished her associate degree and was working a full-time job. She had a boyfriend, *Ian*, and her life was going great. A little over a year later, she came to my condo. She was beside herself because Ian had broken up with her. We stood in my kitchen, and we talked about how the breakup was affecting her. I was standing by the kitchen table, kinda leaning on it with my arms folded, just listening to her. I remember shifting my position, and I put my hand down on the table to brace myself.

As she went on with what happened, I saw her look down at my hand and then look back at me. She described what Ian had said and what she said. Then Tracey looked down a second time. Suddenly, almost mid-sentence, she stopped talking and picked up her purse. I asked what was wrong, and all she said was, "I'm okay, I have to run some errands."

I was surprised. Tracey had gone on and on but hadn't finished what she was saying. I thought maybe she was all talked out, that she didn't want to talk anymore. I told her, okay. She said, "Don't worry, I'm fine. I'll call you later."

About two hours later, I received a call that Tracey was admitted to OSU Hospital. I rushed to the hospital, waited, and waited for the doctor to let me know how she was.

Finally, the doctor said she would be okay, and that she had overdosed on heroin. I was shocked. She had been clean for a year.

After she was back in recovery, I asked her how she could have gone back to drugs? When she told me about Ian and the breakup, she said, she looked down at my hand. She saw a couple of veins sticking out, and it triggered a powerful desire for her to shoot up heroin. The breakup pushed her into a dark tunnel.

The last Mike talked to her; Tracey was clean again. But it taught her mom how even after the addict is in recovery how families must be aware of relapse and how things could pull them back into dark places.

***

Many times, new "How-to" comes from the audience. Two sisters who had recently moved to Columbus from New York City asked to speak to Mike after a lecture. They told him they moved because they wanted to start a new life after overdosing numerous times. They both had gone through in-patient care to get clean. Of course, Mike asked them how they were doing now.

One sister, *Linda*, volunteered; they were doing well.

The other sister, *Lauren*, said, "We wanted to let you know how we were shaving our pills, so you can tell others. We used the metal hose clamps just like you described. We also used metal fingernail files and emery boards to shave down the pills."

Linda continued, "Eventually, we would go into a store and steal pedicure eggs. You know what women used to shave rough skin from their heels? We would put the pills into the shaving part of the ped egg and shave the pills down. All the drugs would be caught at the bottom of the egg."

"It made it really easy to ingest the drug then," finished her sister.

For a free copy of the Indicators of Substance Abuse:

Sandrakhorn.net/Indicators

Acknowledgements

Thank you to all my beta readers, Kathy Clear, Ed Horn, and many individuals who read chapters and offered support on my website. Thank you to my Transition Network friends who have listened to the many chapter versions of *Undercover*.

If writing was the only skill needed to write and publish a book, it would be easier. An online group created by Kathy Ver Eecke titled Pitch to Publish has given me many learning opportunities and support for my efforts. The websites and podcasts of Joanna Penn (The Creative Penn) and K.M. Weiland's Helping Writers Become Authors instructed me in writing and publishing more than many master-level university courses.

Thank you to Michael Powell for believing this book could happen. From the very first time I met Mike at Worthington Kilbourne High School, he has impressed me with his dedication to teaching individuals about the paraphernalia and trends of illegal substances. He served as a consultant to my novel *Downward Spiral*.

Thank you to Shawn Bain for tolerating all the questions I had for him. Shawn instructs individuals on the paraphernalia and trends of illegal substances with Mike. He runs Street Smart Ohio and Global Drug Concepts.

If you would like to reach either Mike or Shawn, you can reach them at info@globaldrugconcepts.com.

Thank you to my readers. My other books can be found on my website, Sandrakhorn.net. I would appreciate you writing a review either on Amazon or Barnes and Noble.

9 798218 077006